COLUMBUS VIGNETTES
II

BILL ARTER

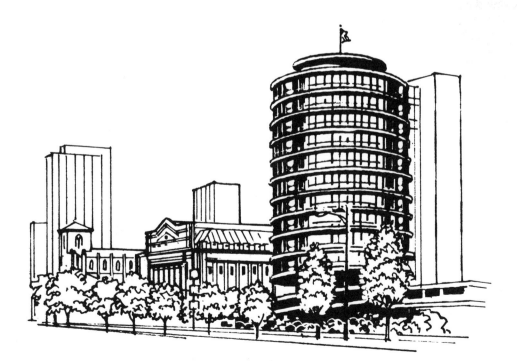

TO MARY

CONTENTS

Note: Numerals after title indicate date originally published.

THIS IS AN occasion of some moment in the annals of the Arters, as I sit down to compose an introduction to a **second** volume of "Columbus Vignettes." The implication — that the first volume was successful — is correct, in a modest way. All of our misgivings and gloomy forebodings were wasted. We are **not** living surrounded by a sea of unsold books as we'd feared. (There is a small remnant of the second printing on hand, but there's plenty of room for the new books when and if they come off the press.) We didn't lose our shirts. We haven't lost our minds — quite.

Now, being worriers by nature, we're worrying about the possibility that Columbusites will have had enough of Vignettes and will resist in great numbers our urging to buy this sequel. If such is the case we may still wind up the only family in town with a huge library — all of the same title. But it's too late to back down. The lithographer is already preparing plates, paper is on hand and the bindery alerted to expect a new job. Wish us luck.

One of the big bonuses that came with our first publishing venture was the mail — letters expressing the pleasure of readers. Many of them came from distant states and foreign countries; from old residents of Columbus who found the book a way to revisit and relive the past. Some few expressed regret at failing to find a favorite landmark. (Many of those missed had been omitted from the first book for lack of space, but are included in this one.)

So much favorable-to-quite-enthusiastic comment came our way that our head has been slightly turned. One result has been a change of attitude. At the risk of being a bore I'll explain:

When I began doing "Columbus Vignettes" for the *Columbus Dispatch Sunday Magazine* (in 1964) I had a sneaky feeling that I was "getting away with murder." I had always loved to look at and explore and draw aging architecture. And I'd always been nosey enough to try learning some of its history. In a fragmentary way I already knew a lot of Columbus lore. When, after forty years of dilettantism, I began putting together the feature for publication, it was almost pure pleasure. And when it developed that a surprising number of readers share my passion, I was awfully pleased. I was also victim of some guilt feelings — for taking money to do what I loved best to do. (I must quickly interpolate for Clyde Long, Editor of the *Sunday Magazine*, that these guilt feelings, so well hidden in the past, have now vanished utterly.) Anyhow, I had the slightly uneasy feeling that I'd stumbled on a racket; that it surely couldn't last.

Lots of nice letters came to Mr. Long and myself from people who read and enjoyed the weekly feature. They helped rid me of my uneasiness. But it was the publication of the book that finished the job. Letters and face-to-face comments included such heart warming thoughts as these: "You are doing a wonderful job in capturing and recording the details of Columbus history" and "Generations to come will thank you for preserving the minutia of local history" or "Don't ever stop adding to what is becoming a most significant collection." I began to walk a wee bit taller.

I had long had the feeling that most recorded history was too entirely concerned with the main stream; dealt too little with the eddies and even puddles that often make history most interesting to non-scholars. Historians can't be blamed. Their self-appointed tasks are nearly always of such a scope that they must stick to large affairs and

omit details. Still, I'd felt, if one had the space to do it in one could reproduce much of the flavor of everyday life in past times. Of course it would take every shelf in the Library of Congress to hold them if books were to contain **all** the detail about **all** the United States. But if one chose a geographic area small enough, say Columbus, Ohio, it would be possible to chronicle small as well as large doings over a considerable period of time.

I won't say that I started with that premise. But, as the series went on, I saw that it was becoming the very thing I'd thought about. To have attempted it as an orderly, chronological account to be completed in one effort, would be a monumental task. Doing it piece at a time, starting and leaving off at any convenient point makes it easier and (I hope) more interesting. The response indicates that the format is a good one.

Anyhow, to finally make the point, I began to view my little stint in a new light. I began to consider myself a "man with a mission" and my small racket as a public service. Now at one end of the pendulum's arc I'll have to swing back to a realization that what I do is at best fragmentary and to a considerable degree ephemeral. My criterion for each piece though is still the same: that it be at least mildly interesting to almost any reader.

I HAVE BEEN making a lot of talks before groups for the past year. Or, more correctly, I've been making essentially one talk before a lot of groups. What I talk about mostly is what interests me most — the Vignettes and my small adventures collecting them. One of the things I often mention is the "Kiss of Death" phenomenon. Not too often, but often enough, a Vignette subject suffers some disaster shortly after publication. (Sometimes it happens before publication, to my disgust.) Early examples include such diverse subjects as the Schumacher Mansion and Schwartz's Castle. Both these were subjects during an earlier incarnation of the Vignettes that I used to do for the Athletic Club magazine, *Blue Wings*.

I talked to Mr. Schumacher about his house (promising not to perpetuate "that ridiculous fence story") and got into print with it. Shortly thereafter Mr. Schumacher died. And shortly after that his fabulous house was razed to the bare ground. Of course Mr. Schumacher's great age, past 90, may have had something to do with his demise.

Frederick Schwartz's person was past any harm from my hexing ability when I first wrote up his "castle" on Third Street just south of Livingston. It was at the time still hemmed in by lesser houses and clutched at by gnarled old trees. I noted in print that it looked like a perfect setting for a murder. Shortly thereafter someone obliged. And within a few months a second murder was done within its gloomy interior.

Then I did the Kappa Kappa Gamma national headquarters house (formerly the Eugene Gray house) on East Town Street. In almost no time a raging fire gutted its beautiful interior.

My Central Markethouse pictures were hardly dry when years of wrangling ended and it was decided to raze it. The drawing was completed but the piece about the Venetian Bridge from the Deshler Hotel to the Lincoln LeVeque tower wasn't finished when it was clawed down. I hastily changed the story and ran it anyway.

The most immediate results came when I drew the Daniel Home, "the Ghost House" at Indianola and East North Broadway. It appeared in the paper on Sunday morning. Through some fluke in printing it looked extra ghostly. Sunday evening, before ten, it was in flames. I was even accused of setting that one to get the front page publicity that resulted.

Not long ago I was talking to a group, recounting some of these kiss-of-death instances when I noticed several women looking pointedly at one of their number, who was looking embarrassed and uneasy. Suddenly I realized it was her 146-year-old house I'd recently used for a Vignette. After the meeting I assured her I had positively not laid a curse on her beautiful home.

Actually, the bad luck my pieces may have brought is outweighed by pleasanter sequels. A number of people have gotten help with their genealogy through mention of names. Others have been put in touch with long-strayed friends and relatives. Still others have been spurred to add to my research about their home and turned up fascinating details.

I'M ALWAYS delighted to have people call to add something to my stories. I'm especially pleased when they write it for that makes a bit of sequel that Clyde Long can use in his "letters column." Phone calls are more common and I wish I could use some of the interesting addenda they provide. One that I remember had to do with the building of O.S.U.'s Armory. The caller told me he was a little boy when it was built. He said the type of brick specified had never been laid by any Columbus mason; that it was finally necessary to import six brick masons from Philadelphia. The six, as befitted imported specialists, lived in the old Neil House. Each morning, he said, they appeared in front of the hotel in cutaway coats, striped pants and **top hats.** They climbed into a carriage that was engaged daily and rode in solemn splendor to the campus. There they doffed their top hats and coats, pulled on aprons and practiced their fine art until quitting time when they returned in state to the Neil House. The picture is unforgettable.

A wealth of minor detail is come by "after the fact." A caller told me an interesting fact after my story appeared about the old interurban station, still standing at Rich and Third. He said the builders were so sanguine about the future of interurbans that the building's foundations and walls were designed to carry ten additional stories. I'm sure they'd have scoffed if anyone had predicted that the fast electric lines had only 18 years to live.

I learn such curiosa as this: The huge William Henry Harrison House replica on the State Fairgrounds was once painted in 12 minutes — by an army of painters ... It was once possible to buy a package deal that was an unbelievable bargain, as follows: My informant said that her mother used to attend the big, flossy summer theater at Olentangy Park for a dollar. The price included train fare to and from Columbus (some 120 miles), streetcar fare to and from the "depot" as well as admission to the park and admission to the theater ... The Indianola Park swimming pool was the "largest in the world" when it was built. Perhaps, at 140 by 238 feet, it never was topped.

I do get some startling *mis*information, such as the solemn assurance by telephone that the old Fred Lazarus home at Bryden and Ohio "had 70 rooms." Robert Lazarus, who grew up in the house, had told me it had 12 rooms plus those on the third floor.

And I get some slightly scandalous information. One bit concerned one of the very large houses that had been heated most economically by gas while that was still considered a very expensive fuel. It seems that the owner had thoughtfully provided two gas lines into his basement, only one of which was routed through his meter.

Among things I didn't choose to believe was an old man's story about his boyhood friend who became one of Columbus' most wildly acclaimed heroes. My informant said he was disgusted with the hero because he came to Columbus to receive a great public greeting — and "didn't even visit his poor old mother."

Some "facts" I've had in advance of writing don't strike me as reliable. An instance was the story of an oldster that he used to play in the empty (of people) Hubbard Mansion at Hubbard and High about 1907. He said all the furniture was in place, in ghostly dust covers and that there was a huge wine cellar still stocked with choicest wines. I didn't use that.

MY DETAILS are sometimes challenged. I told how the builder of a venerable mansion had come to Ohio from Virginia, in 1817, with a passel of slaves. A descendent of the gentleman in question said quite positively that he never owned a slave in his life. Since it all happened 150 years ago it's impossible to prove either version.

FIRST BISHOP CHASE HOME · WORTHINGTON

I had quite a time over the residence of Bishop Philander Chase at High and Selby — where Kenyon College began. I was hooted at by a writer who said the Bishop **never** lived in it; that it was built long after his death. An exchange of letters, one from a former owner, offered equally positive evidence that I was right. In the course of my checking I did discover an earlier Chase home, still standing at 67 Lincoln Avenue. Here is my sketch of it. The other, which appears in this book is reasonably well authenticated as the site of pre-Kenyon classes held by Chase. The question becomes academic as plans go forward to raze the High Street house.

One interesting fact came to light long after my piece on Franklin Park Conservatory appeared. I had learned that the building was originally erected at the Chicago World's Fair, the Columbian Exposition of 1893, but I couldn't learn how it got to Columbus. Mr. Clyde Eide wrote to me that he had found the 1902 catalog of a wrecking company which states, "The Chicago House Wrecking Company was organized with the avowed intention and purpose of dismantling and purchasing large institutions and expositions. Our first undertaking of any note was the purchase of the World's Fair (Columbian) of

Chicago. This mammoth institution which cost in the neighborhood of $33,000,000 to erect was purchased by us for $80,000." It further states that the enterprising company prepared and issued a catalog giving detailed specifications of all exposition material and distributed 500,000 copies. Mr. Eide concluded that some Columbusite received a catalog and began a drive to bring the ornate conservatory to Columbus where it stands today.

I MENTIONED earlier that some of the first year's Vignettes (1964) are included in this volume. One of that few demonstrates the vulnerability of my subjects. The title is "Status Symbol" and it deals with the great coach house behind the old Hoster Mansion on East Rich. As we started preparing this book we checked and found the mansion and its attendant coachhouse standing solidly as Gibraltar. But just last week I drove by and found both leveled. This set me to searching for sketches made years ago of two other coach houses now no more.

THE HARTMAN CARRIAGE HOUSE

They were the gigantic horse, carriage and coachman quarters behind the old Hartman House on Town Street and Frederick Schumacher's coach house. It has seemed to me that these monstrous affairs devoted to horse drawn transport epitomized a vanished way of life for the wealthy as no other structures could. The sketches are reproduced here. Incidentally they are testimony to the validity of the argument I give Mary about not throwing things away. If you keep 'em long enough you'll find a use for them.

Whilst arranging the older Vignettes for publication I was struck by the comparative crudeness of some of the drawings. I hadn't realized that I was fussing more and more over them as time went on. Some of the oldest were so poor by contrast that I redrew them — seven or eight in all. Which may explain to anyone who saved the older ones why the pictures are different.

This is a good place to mention that I have once more put the dates of original publication after the titles on the "Contents" page.

THIS MAY ALSO be a good place to address an apology to some people whose efforts I greatly appreciate even though it hasn't yet become apparent. These are the people who have made suggestions for excellent Vignettes which I have not yet acted upon. I still get a steady flow,

SCHUMACHER'S COACH HOUSE

many of which are entirely appropriate. Some of them are readily researched, get written and soon appear in print. Others, equally good, take a lot longer because some essential facts are so hard to come by. Most of them are being developed a bit at a time. Keeping them in "open file" is often most fruitful. Odd facts often crop up as I research other subjects or as I interview some old timer. Most of them will eventually be written. To those who wonder what happened to their suggestions, I offer this explanation and my apologies.

And this is the place for thanks. The list would be endless if I tried to make it at all complete. To the hundreds who have given me leads or helped me with facts, my heartfelt thanks. I couldn't possibly keep up the series without your assistance.

Again I want to thank Herb Byer and Gus Bowman for both encouragement and forbearance. I continue to pile up indebtedness to my wonderful librarian friends who help dig out obscure facts (and who, to my intense pleasure, bought an astonishing number of the first book for personal copies).

My wife, Mary, and our girls, Kacy and Beth, are helping even more to get this volume put together, for which I publicly thank them.

All of the credit for beautiful reproduction in the first book is due to Del Nida, Eddie Eckstein and their talented staff of lithographers. I hope they read this before proceding with the reproduction of the second set of drawings so they'll be inspired to do an equally superb job.

And a huge "Thanks!" to all the people who laid out a considerable sum to buy Volume One. We can't express strongly enough our gratitude to you, many hundreds of whom we may never know.

The question, "Will there be other volumes of Vignettes?" is unanswerable except with "ifs." If the perpetrator (meaning me) lives and is able to keep going and if Editor Long is willing to publish them, the *Sunday Magazine* feature will continue. If this volume pays its way and if publishing costs don't go up too much more — then there will probably be more bound books; at least until someone hollers, "uncle!"

Bill Arter
Worthington, Ohio

August, 1967

Traveling Statue

QUITE a contrast is presented by the crisp, contemporary styling of the Columbus Health Department building and a rather quaint statue which graces its lawn. The curious may learn, from the statue's pedestal, that this is a "Memorial Fountain" honoring Samuel Michael Smith and his sons. The date is 1880. Sure enough, one notes, there is a basin-like projection, now filled, that must have been the fountain. But who was Smith and how came he to this location? A little research turned up the answers.

Dr. S. M. Smith was one of Columbus' leading physicians in mid-19th century, professor and later dean of Starling Medical College and surgeon-general of Ohio during the Civil War.

Along with other more or less distinguished citizens of his day he might have been entirely forgotten. His wife and daughters planned otherwise. Six years after his death, in 1874, they had this statue made and erected. With the city's permission it was placed at Broad and High streets at the southeast corner. It stood there, actually out in Broad, until 1900. Then, because it was interfering with traffic, it was moved to the grounds of the still active Starling Medical College (old St. Francis Hospital). When that venerable structure was razed, in 1957, Dr. Smith took another trip, this time to his present pleasant location.

The sculptor, William Walcutt, was most successful in a family of artists. Columbus-born and reared, he studied abroad for many years and then returned. Among his other work is a statue of Commodore Perry in Cleveland. In later years Walcutt went to New York where he became a government expert at the Port of New York, appraising works of art imported into this country.

The Smith monument incorporates relief portraits of the doctor's two sons designed as medallions. The good doctor himself stands quietly, his eyes fixed on a point northeast. Perhaps he misses his old hangout and keeps wondering what's going on at Broad and High.

Schiller Park

STEWART'S Grove, south of the city, was a favorite spot for 19th century Columbusites, especially the Germans who flocked to Columbus in the 1850s and 1860s. Their "village" of neat, brick cottages extended toward the beautiful grove, and many German affairs — *Saengerbunde,* gymnastic exhibitions and club parades—began or ended under its trees.

In 1867 the city bought the 23.59-acre grove from Messrs. Deshler and Thurman for $15,000. It was promptly named "City Park," a name still retained by the street along its western edge. Within five years, it had its winding drives and walks, an ornamental fountain, a lake (with an artificial hill as a by-product) and one live eagle with a wingspread of eight and one-half feet. The eagle had been captured in Madison County. It proved a most popular attraction.

City Park, in time, was surrounded by the German community. The grateful burghers decided to grace it with a statue. July 4, 1891, saw the festive unveiling. German-American hearts swelled as the bronze figure of the great German poet, Friedrich Schiller, was revealed. It had been fashioned and cast in bronze, in far-off Munich, Germany, at a cost of $3000. Pedestal and statute stood an impressive 25 feet high.

The park was renamed Schiller to everyone's satisfaction. But then came the war—World War I. A hysterical wave of anti-German bitterness swept the country. Everything German was hated, hooted and abused. Schiller Park was declared renamed—to Washington Park—and attempts were made to destroy the statue.

In later, saner years the city fathers decried that period, and the park resumed the name Schiller. The poet still stands, unruffled by his period of disgrace, at the west entrance to the park.

I sketched a neck of the pretty lake, looking toward the park's shelterhouse.

BILL ARTER

Union Station

"THE Union Depot is one of the largest and best arranged in the West, and 100 passenger trains come and go each day. The railroads, of course, run their tracks where they please—across the streets and thoroughfares, without regard to the comfort or cost to the city; but, as railroads go, they are considerate, and when they run over a streetcar, a cab, or a citizen they usually express regret." Thus wrote historian Henry Howe in 1887. He referred to the second of Columbus' three union stations. The first was frame with three tracks, built in the 1850s.

The second station was built in 1872, at grade and with a maze of tracks that literally cut Columbus in two. By 1875 public clamor had caused the digging of a tunnel under all the tracks at a cost of $45,000. After the novelty wore off it was used only by horsecars. Others braved the grade crossing rather than endure the darkness and stench of the tunnel.

Then, in 1895, the present viaduct was completed at a cost of $369,000, and the grand "Union Depot" was begun. The classic, neo-Roman station was designed by Daniel H. Burnham, architectural titan of the World's

Columbian Exposition and designer of celebrated buildings all over America. It was completed in 1897 and cost $750,000. Part of its majestic, arched facade along High Street has been torn down, but its fine lines can still impress. When completed it was called "The World's Finest" (locally at least).

Before the Third Street viaduct was built, few persons ever had seen the Union Station as it can be seen from that structure. Recently I parked in the old railroad yard and trudged back to the center of the bridge. There was a real fascination in seeing the familiar old building from so unfamiliar a vantage point.

The big concourse is seen to be a long shed with the covered stairways that lead to track level looking like four playground sliding boards. The main building is grander even than one might suppose from the inside. The tracks curve away beyond the station and duck under High Street like varmints going into holes. It was well worth the trip.

Then I got started on the sketch. As I worked, sitting on my little stool, a carload of youngsters slowed beside me. Amid their laughter I heard "Must be some kinda nut."

Dr. Goodale's Good Deed

MAJOR Nathan Goodale, as an officer in the American Revolution, got land in Ohio. Part of it was what later became the most celebrated river island in America — Blennerhasset. It was while plowing the island's flood-enriched soil that he disappeared, forever, apparently a victim of prowling Indians. That was in 1792, when his son Lincoln was 10 years old. Not long afterward young "Linc" began to read medicine with old Doc Jewett of Belpre.

At 23 Linc had moved on to the thriving village of Franklinton. In those days, doctors didn't do well financially, but young Goodale covered two bases. He opened Columbus' (or Franklinton's) first pharmacy and prospered mightily. Even so, he'd never have become so rich but for his faith in the future of Columbus. He bought liberal hunks of the wilderness that surrounded him and profited as those on the ground floor often are able to do. The War of 1812 was only a temporary setback. Goodale was one of the first volunteers. When he returned, a capital city had been decreed across the river, and the value of his investments increased tenfold.

In 1851, out of gratitude, he dedicated "40 acres adacent to the north boundary of the city . . . well worth $40,000 . . . untouched by axe or plow." He gave it as a park, the first for Columbus. By 1852 the city had enclosed it and cleared away the brush. It was a magnificent forest of virgin beech, maple and oak. Nine years later came the Civil War, and Goodale Park became Camp Jackson, where recruits slept on donated straw and drilled among the trees.

In 1872, four years after Goodale's death, a growing Columbus lavished attention on the neglected park — laid out carriage drives, dug a lake and embellished it with a fountain. In 1888 one of America's celebrated sculptors, Urbana-born J. Q. A. Ward, was commissioned to design a suitable memorial to the park's donor. Ward has many famous works in Washington and New York. His superior genius is clearly demonstrated in the bust of Goodale, visible through the gateway in the sketch.

BILL ARTER

Flatiron Building

O NE of Columbus' oddest structures stands on a tiny pie-shaped plot facing North Fourth Street at Naghten Street. Its other two sides are hugged by Locust and Lazelle streets. Its smallest side—but its principal facade, architecturally—is barely eight feet wide but an impressive four stories high. The structure was built by one of Columbus' best-loved Irishmen.

The builder's name and the date, "H. A. HIGGINS 1914," are carved in a stone which still crowns the structure. His given name was Herbert Aloysius, but to everyone he was "Myrt." Here's why:

At six he started to school at venerable St. Patrick's. His mother's pride was his long, golden curls which he wore, all unsuspecting, to school. The "young ruffians" at St. Pat's delightedly dubbed him "Myrtle" and so humiliated him that he ran home vowing never to return. His big sister, Mary, soon got at the truth and, risking maternal hysterics, whisked him to a barber to be shorn. Next day short-haired Herbert got a shortened nickname. They dubbed him "Myrt" and it stuck all his life.

The little flatiron building, built while he was still a youth, was largely his own conception. With a saloon in the narrow end, a grocery in the wide end (25 feet) and apartments above, young Myrt was, indeed, an entrepeneur.

Business boomed the first year as the new Fourth Street viaduct was being built. Construction men and railroad men thronged his place. His beautiful solid-cherry bar was seldom empty. People liked the place, and they liked the proprietor, whose kindness, wit and generosity were legends. When circuses loaded in the B. and O. yards Myrt stayed open all hours to accommodate the show folk. Needy neighbors could always count on a bit of credit to tide them over a tight spot. Prohibition changed the saloon to a restaurant, but still it was a favorite spot for Irishmen and others.

When Myrt Higgins died in 1943 he was mourned by all who knew him. They tell of the first St. Patrick's Day parade after his death. It formed, as usual, at the Irish saint's own church and marched down Naghten. As the marchers came opposite the wedge-shape building they paused. Hats came off, and a moment of silence for Myrt was observed before the parade moved on.

Progress

CITY expressways are, without doubt, essential to a populace on wheels. They cut through congestion like a shaft of light through a dark room. But they are ruthless, too. In the process of cutting seconds off traveling time, they often cut former thoroughfares and make dead ends of old familiar streets. Lifelong patterns of living and business are shattered.

No one knows this better than Pat Salvatore. His neighborhood market was established at 77 East Russell Street 43 years ago. It was, and still is, located in the tall, narrow building shown in the foreground of the sketch. Before the Goodale Interchange was built, this was a most flourishing location. The building itself, four tall floors and a heavy cornice high, has been a landmark since before the turn of the century. Old-time residents remember when a dance hall occupied its third story. The natural trading area of the store ran eastward to North Fourth Street, as did the fated Russell Street itself. Now that considerable section extending from Pat's to North Fourth

might as well be across town. The freeway and the Third Street extension have effectively sealed it off and dried up much of its trade. Pat is philosophical about it. He agrees that part of the price of progress is paid by those in the path of improvements.

The neighborhood, today, has a quiet, cut-off atmosphere, merely accentuated by the sight and sound of traffic on Third, high above the little street. From my balcony seat on the bridge I could watch traffic from the Third Street off-ramp joining traffic from Fourth and both merging with the interchange before passing under High Street. Looking past the store and Kerr Street, I could glimpse busy High and, far beyond, the huge, nearly completed Thurber Towers apartment building at Neil and Goodale. Though a quarter mile away, its crisp, contemporary lines dominate the distant scene.

Almost all the land within my view was "William Neil's Addition, layed off in lots" when that tycoon was at the height of his tycooning (hotel, stagecoaches and real estate) in the mid-19th century.

Flour Mill Phoenix

LIKE the fabled Phoenix, this vast mill has risen thrice from ashes. By coincidence, it was a retired fireman, Louis Heinmiller, who turned in the first alarm at 11:13 p.m. on Saturday, November 3, 1945. Within minutes the towering Gwinn Mill, Main Street landmark, was going up in spectacular flames. By 12:50 practically all fire equipment in Columbus was at the scene. Twenty thousand spectators clogged the area, in spite of an earlier explosion that had knocked at least one spectator a hundred feet.

Just past midnight the four-story mill building collapsed and the tinder-like maze of granaries and chutes fed flames visible for seven miles. The fire was not pronounced extinguished until Monday morning. Only the towering concrete bins remained. Night Watchman M. R. Barrett died of burns. Damage was estimated at more than a million dollars.

The mill had been built in 1908 by O. E. Gwinn. Its location was farmland, outside the city limits. It was one of the largest in America and its product, Jefferson Flour, was shipped everywhere. Just a short distance up Nelson Road had been the old Nelson Mill, built in 1832 and powered by the waters of Alum Creek. The Gwinn Mill was steam powered from the start.

After the fire, President Clarence E. Gwinn decided to rebuild. It took 20 months and the newly-built mill operated just 20 hours when the second big fire struck, early in the morning, July 4, 1947. Again it was a general alarm fire. Again an explosion occurred, and again the big mill collapsed. Fortunately the 1¼-million-bushel storage space was less than a quarter full. Damage still ran to half a million dollars. Mr. Gwinn ordered the mill rebuilt again.

In August, 1949, the third fire broke out. It was started when a welding torch ignited hexane fumes. (Hexane was used in soy bean processing, no longer done at the mill.) This third and last fire did the smallest damage but still was estimated at $200,000. Firemen were praised for their efficiency in saving most of the property.

Continental Grain Company, present owners, bought the huge facility in 1950. It is said to be one of the two or three largest grain firms in the world. With recent additions the Columbus bins can store about two million bushels of grain. The drawing was made from the little parkway that bisects Bulen Avenue. Most Columbusites see the big installation from Main Street, but its immense bulk can best be realized from the south.

17

The Cove

FOR more years than I care to contemplate, I have trod the streets and byways of Columbus always with an eye for the picturesque and with curiosity about the unusual. For most of that time it has been a hobby to make drawings of the things that interested me. By degrees I found that at least some other persons were interested in the same things.

It seemed desirable to append to the pictures some sprightly and informative text—if only to justify publishing the drawings. Since the text could hardly be mere variations on the theme, "I liked its looks, so I drew it," I had to do some, and sometimes considerable, research.

It would be most gratifying if *Sunday Magazine* readers would suggest candidates for this series. Likely subjects would include buildings (especially if they have interesting histories or notable associations), places, vistas, sections, fragments or almost anything that can be drawn by a

middling draftsman and written about with some authority. It would be especially helpful if I could be directed to sources for the facts needed. I'd be inclined to favor suggestions made by more than one person, an indication of the popularity of the subject.

Oh, yes, about the structure in the accompanying sketch . . . "I liked its looks, so I drew it." I've called it "The Cove," because it is sheltered by the cliff-like walls of bigger buildings. Curiously rural looking, it lies within a couple of blocks of the city's center. A sort of "Topsy House" that just grew, its materials include clapboard, shingles, brick, concrete and river boulders. Its rooflines (and all its lines, for that matter) are whimsical, to say the least. In summer it is shaded by trees in bundles and clumps that grew as casually as the house itself. It is located along narrow, Downtown Oak Street between Fifth and Sixth streets.

The 'Shot Tower'

THE Civil War was still raging and the North had lost its illusions about a quick victory when ground was broken for the "Old Shot Tower." It was October, 1863. Munitions were desperately needed on the several fronts and round, lead shot led the list of wants. But how could a tower help?

A British plumber discovered the shot-tower principle. In practice, molten lead was hoisted by windlass to the top of a high tower. There it was discharged into a sieve-like pan. The pan was struck repeated blows causing blobs of lead to drop. At the base of the tower was a vat of water into which the drops of lead fell and solidified. Round shot resulted without further effort.

The site of the tower had been bought from the Neil family for $16,000. It consisted of approximately 77 acres along the Old Harbor Road, now Cleveland Avenue. It was called the Columbus Arsenal and the shot tower was its first structure. It was completed and operating precisely a century ago. The three-story main building was com-

pleted the following year. In 1875 the Arsenal was transferred to the Recruiting Service in time to enlist men for the Indian wars. Officially it was the Columbus Recruiting Depot but to Columbus folk it was always "the Barracks". About 1900, 7.9 acres were deeded to the city to widen and improve Cleveland, Buckingham and Jefferson Avenues.

The parklike grounds became a favorite resort of local citizens who picnicked there, strolled along the shores of Lake Lulu (named, it is said, for a commanding officer's daughter) and listened, enthralled, to band concerts. Buildings continued to be erected as needed. At last count there were 141 of all types. In 1922 the complex was named Fort Hayes in honor of former President Rutherford Hayes. Recent announcement of plans to abandon the Fort caused a scramble to acquire the site. Presently a "Save Fort Hayes committee" is hoping to persuade the federal government to continue to operate the century-old facility.

The Ohio Pen

BACK in the 1920s, most visitors to Columbus sought the shivery thrill of a tour through the Ohio Penitentiary. The throng of visitors kept close ranks as they visited a cell block, the dining room, chapel, yard and, finally, the Death House with its electric chair. The tours ended in 1930 after the greatest of many pen fires killed 320 convicts. The ancient structure was on the eve of its 100th birthday.

The land, near the confluence of the Scioto and Olentangy Rivers, was acquired in 1832 and consisted of 15 acres purchased for $800. Two years later the new pen was occupied. Its 24-foot walls enclosed some six acres and the principal building was 400 feet long. Most of it still stands. After an addition in 1837, the cost was $93,370 plus 1,113,462 convict-days of labor.

For many years convict labor was a commodity eagerly bought by contractors. In 1884 the list of contracts was long: The Hayden Shops made ironwork, Brown & Hinman made garden tools; others were the Columbus Boot & Shoe, Ohio Tool, Geo. W. Gill Stove Foundry & Finishing Shop, Ayers & Mithoff, woodwork for carriages and the Evans & Mithoff Toy Shop. Hardest, most hated work was the Patton foundry and grinding whereas the nicest work was to be found in the chair shop.

Punishment in earlier days was inflicted at the whipping post and in dunking tubs. A later, more refined device was the "hummingbird," a large box where the prisoner was confined in 18 inches of water and subjected first to a blast of steam and subsequently to an electric shock. Observers wrote that "Prisoners beg piteously to avoid a second dose."

The final horror was the work of three prisoners who, on the night of April 21, 1930, turned the pen into an inferno that roared toward doomed men in locked cells as they screamed for help in vain. The three had arranged a candle, floating on a chip in a bucket of kerosene. They expected it to ignite at dinnertime. The fire came after the men were locked in their cells for the night. The final count was 320 dead (some by suicide) and 230 hospitalized. A whole nation was shocked and sickened by the horror of that night. Ironically, damage to the building was estimated at a mere $11,000.

My sketch was made from the south side of Spring Street.

Glen Echo

COLUMBUS is one of the most nearly level cities east of the prairie country. From its highest point to its lowest is only 191 feet. The high point, elevation 893.347 feet, is at Karl Road and Elmore Avenue. The low point, 702.347 feet, is at Glenwood and Thomas Avenues. Note by the figures that "flat" does not mean "low" as some visitors assume. Actually Columbus is on a relatively high plateau within shouting distance of 1000 feet above sea level. The official elevation of the city is 777.601 feet, as is attested to by a marker on the northeast corner of the Courthouse.

Nevertheless, people of our city have a largely unsatisfied hunger for hills and valleys. Little Glen Echo Park provides both in a confined but satisfying dose. The park itself, with an area of 3.90 acres, consists of the bed and tiny valley of Glen Echo Run—a now-you-see-it, now-you-don't stream which is underground for much of its course to the Olentangy River.

Picturesque bridges, nice tables and fine trees set in grassy plots make pastoral vignettes against a backdrop of shaly cliffs or wooded banks. Its special prettiness is worth a visit.

Columbus was feeling its oats in 1912 when the park was acquired—its centennial year. Still there was probably no connection between the events. More likely the Columbus Real Estate & Improvement Company pushed the deal to further its own plans. At least that firm conveyed most of the present site to the city. In 1929 a small addition was purchased for $1000. It is presumed that the real estate men developed some of the adjacent residential streets including Parkview Drive, Glen Echo, Cliffside and Glenmawr.

For many years after making it a park, the city had virtually abandoned it. Rough roadways led to the park from North Fourth and Glen Echo, but it lay almost a wilderness below the busy streets around it. Small boys found it ideal for daytime fun. Then, during 1962 and 1963, the city cleaned, refurbished and built necessary facilities to make it the jewel it is today.

One portion is no longer accessible by car. It is seen in my sketch. The handsome bridge with its theatrical stone staircase, carries Indianola Avenue over the gorge. Looking, among the trees, like a classic ruin, its underpass is now closed by a barrier.

Fourth Street School

FOR THE first time since automobiles were invented, motorists traveling north on Fourth Street have a clear view of old Fourth Street School's facade. A study in contrasts, my sketch was made from the south end of the new viaduct over the brand new freeway. Construction of these has swept away all intervening structures.

In old school records it is called the Fulton Street German-English School. It was a genuinely bilingual institution. Two buildings once occupied the site; one was built in 1862, the other, in 1871. It is assumed the one still standing is the younger—just short of a century old. The school report for 1862 shows a Columbus student enrollment of 3189, with 11 buildings and 48 teachers. Among interesting statistics for that year, school receipts were $58,274 while expenditures were only $29,763.

Alfred Hensley, a student at Old Fourth from 1906 to 1913, told me that in his day both buildings were used, the older for the first seven grades and the other for eighth grade, assembly hall and Principal Pfeiffer's office. He spoke nostalgically of the old gang: "Heinie" Mead, who later pitched for the old Columbus Senators, Sammie Trott, the boxer, Charles and Dewey Grell and Freddie Wilhelm. Fifth Street boys included Joe and Bobby Shaefer, the Brehl boys and Bill Erlenbach. Over on Livingston Avenue were Bill and Jim McNamara and Frank and Harry Schmidt. Lawrence Bower, who was so intelligent he was nicknamed "Brainy," lived on Sixth Street but was the acknowledged leader of the "Fifth Street Gang."

In its nearly 100 years, the old school has been host to thousands of other students, each remaining fondly in the memory of classmates. The building was abandoned as a school in 1953 when the beautiful, new Mohawk School was completed. Old Fourth Street School is now owned and used as storage space by the Heer Printing Company. The old playground, once scene of noisy fun, now serves as a parking lot for the company.

A Century and A Third

ON JANUARY 23, 1931, St. John's Episcopal Church in Worthington began its second hundred years, now just one third gone. The church congregation was organized in 1804, having been agreed upon in 1802 before Worthington's settlers left Granby, Connecticut. Familiar names are found on the list of original officers: James Kilbourne, Ezra Griswold, Abner Pinney and others. Church services were held in the log building which served as both school and church, as well as town hall. James Kilbourne was the first rector. In 1817, Philander Chase, founder of Kenyon College and first Episcopal Bishop of Ohio, became rector.

The present building was begun in 1827. Most of the work was done by members. Stone for the foundation came from the vinicity — from Rush Creek and Whetstone River and from the fields nearby. The timber list will make a person interested in refurbishing antiques drool: "105 sawlogs, all very fine, viz. 20 cherry, 18 butternut,

and the balance 67 black walnut." The brick was fired close to the site, wrought iron nails were made by hand and the lath was split with an axe.

The church is practically as it was 133 years ago. An addition to the rear, as seen in my sketch, was made in 1917 and the tower has been rebuilt for safety, but the old walnut pulpit is still in use and the stones in the old burying ground continue to stand as they have since the church was new.

The original incorporators of the village set apart the town lot on the village green as the site of their church. They also set apart 100 acres of farm land for its support. That acreage remained farm land until half a dozen years ago when it was sold, subdivided and built upon. Today it is the Worthington section called Kilbourne Village.

My sketch was made from across Granville Road (in the elementary schoolyard) looking toward the village green and High Street.

Status Symbol

THERE is much to recommend alley prowling—particularly behind the once-fashionable residential streets of the city. The rewards for traveling these byways may be close-up views of old coach houses.

More than the house itself, the coach house is a clue to the opulent way of life enjoyed by very wealthy persons of the nineteenth century. Even well-to-do families in days before automobiles made do without private transportation. Merely owning, maintaining and housing as simple an outfit as one horse and buggy took a tremendous bite out of the city man's income. To own a passable pair and a decent "rig" was far beyond the means of most. If one aspired to fine, matched teams and carriages, a coachman and a groom or two had to be counted as unavoidable expense. And horses, rolling stock and employes all had to be housed. The coach house became visible evidence of huge wealth—a status symbol comparable to today's private multi-engine airplane and hired pilot.

Even so, Columbus' better alleys once were studded with grand structures devoted to gracious, horse-drawn transport. Many were as large and elegant as some of the finest houses. A notable one at Town Street and Washington Avenue, coach house of the late Peruna-medicine-king, S. B. Hartman, was recently razed. Of white brick, three stories high and huge enough to house a dozen teams, carriages and sleighs, as well as an army of grooms, it sported leaded glass windows and ornate stone carving.

Its near neighbor, still standing at 555 East Rich Street, is behind the old Hoster home. Some 75 feet long, only a portion is seen in my sketch. Like the great house it served, it is built of massive stone and sports the same rare, curved mansard roof. Upper windows are topped by classic pediments and framed in fancy, carved pilasters. The doors are heavy and are high enough to admit the carriages.

House and coach house were built about 1890 by a famous brewing tycoon. The scale of the house is monumental as indicated by its third-floor ballroom which has served as an auditorium seating 400 people. The formal garden to the east once had a beautiful fountain (the ruin is visible in the sketch) that was graced with a costly marble statuary group imported from abroad.

Whose Castle?

MANY a visitor, traveling Columbus' West Broad Street, has been struck by the enchanting distant view of these towers and stiletto-like spires. Such admiration has been evoked ever since they were erected in 1868.

Now called the State School, it was once known as the Ohio Institution for Feeble Minded Youth. The land it stands upon, "fair and high, two and a half miles west of the capitol," was purchased just 100 years ago. Most of the 187 acres cost $35 an acre in that Civil War year.

When the buildings were completed, it was said they were "without equal on this planet." Whoever the architect was, he had a fine feeling for the romantic embroidery of the Neo-Gothic period. A puzzle developed as I sought facts: All records say that the principal building was totally destroyed by fire in 1881 (fortunately without any injuries) yet old engravings show the 1868 structure almost exactly like the one standing. The one difference is the lack of a tallish spire rising from the top of the square

tower. The most likely explanation is that the building's interior was burned out but that the heavy walls remained. The missing spire may have been of wood that burned and was not replaced in the reconstruction.

The original building, designed for 300 students, was soon crowded. By the time of the fire, it and some additions housed 614 people. As of April, 1964, there were 2250 residents. Needless to say, there have been many new buildings added in the meantime. The current report lists 41 residence units; the great number permit those of like age and ability to be together. The total number of employes is 875, including service workers, teachers, medical, technical and nursing staff. An active rehabilitation program has been greatly aided by the newest building (foreground) devoted to "activities therapies."

The picture, unlike others in this series, is a watercolor painting. I worked on the wide lawn a few yards west of the driveway.

25

City Cross-Section

Here is one of those fascinating cross-sections in Columbus that spans a century of architecture. The scene caught my eye while strolling south on Grant Avenue, just past the Columbus Public Library. The unusual view was made possible by the razing of the very oldest portion of old Grant Hospital. Its removal revealed fragments more ancient than itself—like the old soft-brick house (with two modern ventilating stacks) that dates back to Civil War times. It was part of a fine home which sat well back from State Street. It now serves as an appendage to a comparatively recent business building that runs to the sidewalk's edge.

Beyond it is the Medical Arts Building at 327 East State Street. Built in the twenties, it is made of that era's favorite material, wire-cut brick. Still further beyond, dwarfing the once tall Medical Arts Building, is the strikingly contemporary new Grant Hospital. Of glittering glass and white brick, it forms an incongruous backdrop for its neighbors. It's almost as though one stage set is still in place as another is being readied in the background.

Grant Hospital, which once stood where cars are parked, was founded by Dr. James Fairchild Baldwin in 1900. It was at the time the largest private hospital in the world and its proud boast was, "Bathrooms are found on *each floor!*"

Far older was neighboring St. Francis Hospital that stood where Grant Hospital now stands. Its foundations were laid in 1849 on the margin of a dismal swamp which lay between Fourth and Sixth streets. The old building, literally encrusted with medieval ornament and crowned with castle-like towers, was built as Starling Medical College. OSU's College of Medicine may be traced back to the old school.

In 1865, the Sisters of the Poor of St. Francis leased half the huge building to establish their hospital. The school and the hospital shared quarters until 1914 when the hospital took over all the space. It was closed in 1955 and was knocked down the next year in order to make way for the marvelous new Grant Hospital, a unique cruciform building that makes maximum use of the restricted space.

Urban Preserval

READING over the thick, old abstract on this property at 538 East Town Street is like reading history. Its first page deals with the results of conscience pangs suffered by our Revolutionary leaders.

When the American Colonies rebelled against England, they found sympathy and aid forthcoming from British subjects in the provinces to the north. Those who openly supported the American Colonies were driven from their homes and were forced to take refuge among the colonists. As early as 1783, our Congress promised to make amends for their losses. It was 1798 before refugees were invited to present claims for their losses, to be repaid in what Congress had the most of—land. To satisfy the claims, the so-called "Refugee Tract" was created. Of 100,000 acres, it included much of what became Franklin County.

In 1802, Thomas Jefferson conveyed a parcel of the land to refugee John Allen. It included the site on Town Street. Allen apparently never visited his holdings or paid taxes, for the land was sold to Lyne Starling by the sheriff in 1809. Starling, with three partners, founded Columbus on the land they acquired. The city was just nicely established when William Neil (of stagecoach and tavern fame) entered the scene in 1827. He had secured a quit-claim deed from Allen's heirs and challenged Starling's title. Starling engaged no lesser light than Henry Clay to do battle with Neil. After three years, Starling finally won.

The Town Street land was bought by Benjamin L. Kelly, who started to build the house in the foreground in 1844. He was soon in trouble as the B. Comstock Company sought to foreclose to satisfy a $600 debt (at 12 per cent interest). The house was sold by Sheriff John Graham to Francis Crum. In 1865, the house and surrounding land were acquired by John Bartlet who laid it out in lots as "University Addition."

In 1932, the house was sold by the executor for Henry D. Turney to the Keever Starch Company. Later the company bought the house to the east, restored both magnificently and joined them with an addition. Today the handsome homes serve admirably as offices for National Industrial Products Company, which includes Keever and Exact Weight Scale Company. A spokesman for the firm says he enjoyed the remark of one of his friends, that theirs was a job of "urban renewal without bulldozer or boondoggle." It should be an inspiration to others who would preserve our heritage of architecture without public assistance.

27

The Frog Pond

COLUMBUS of the mid-nineteenth century was still a very small city. Its population in 1850 was less than twenty thousand. Most citizens found it no chore to walk to any point in town, a mere matter of minutes within its compact environs.

The level plain which began at High Street and ran eastward to the horizon seemed made for easy plotting and building. And it was, except for one thing: Much of the area within the corporation was swampy and unfit for use without major engineering. Joel Wright's city plat of 1812 shows a vast "no man's land" extending from Fourth Street eastward half a mile or more. This, according to most evidence, was land too swampy to be sold for lots.

Bit by bit the land was reclaimed by draining. One of the earliest and most spectacular jobs was done by famous Alfred Kelley. He bought all the land from Broad to Long and from Fifth to Seventh Streets. (Seventh has been renamed Grant Avenue.) He had 918 feet frontage on Broad for which he paid just $917. There, in 1837, he built his Greek Revival mansion. When it was torn down recently remnants of his great drainage tunnel were found. It had made his bargain land an ideal estate.

But, as late as 1848, one great morass still existed in the near-Downtown area. It stretched from near Fourth Street to Sixth Street, south of Broad. Starling Loving described it as, "a swamp or pond in which were several large elms, relics of the original forest. It was the home of noisy frogs, the breeding place of *Plasmodium Malariae* and in winter afforded capital skating for boys."

When the trustees of the projected Starling Medical College were looking for a site, citizens objected to having it near their homes. For that reason, and because the land was cheap, it was built on a plot along the eastern edge of the pond. There were no near neighbors. The building stood for 108 years and then was razed to make way for the new Grant Hospital. The stretch of East State Street in my sketch includes the area where the old pond lay. Closing the vista is the white marble City Library. At left is the former Knights of Columbus Building with the Charminel Hotel just beyond and Grant Hospital opposite. On the site of the Knights of Columbus Building stood the home of Dr. Francis Carter, once Dean of the Medical College. It was later the home of Governor Salmon P. Chase and the scene of ill-fated Kate Chase's first social triumphs.

No one seems to know precisely when the "frog pond" disappeared. Most likely it was gradually filled as houses crept eastward from Fourth until one day it was no more.

Where Kenyon Began

I F LOCAL tradition is to be trusted, this house at North High Street and Selby Boulevard was the home of Bishop Philander Chase. Its site is, without question, the edge of the bishop's 150-acre farm, now largely occupied by the Chaseland and Colonial Hills sections of Worthington.

Philander (a curious name for a bishop) came to pioneer Worthington in 1817. He took charge of the local academy and, it is said, held classes in his home. Thus, this house may be considered the principal root of Kenyon College which Chase founded in 1826.

During his first year here, the bishop labored on his farm to augment his small earnings. He also accepted, in lieu of cash, labor by his students. His nephew, Salmon Chase, lived here, helping on the farm and furthering his education. He later became Governor of Ohio, Secretary of the Treasury and a Supreme Court Justice.

Bishop Chase preached the first Episcopal service in Columbus in 1817. After the service, 30 persons associated themselves as the "Parish of Trinity Church," thus founding the church that has worshipped a hundred years at Broad and Third streets. Chase continued to officiate both in Columbus and at St. John's in Worthington. And he continued to dream of a "western" college to prepare

young men for the ministry in frontier communities. In 1825, he sailed to England seeking funds for such a school. He was very successful. Largest contributors were Lord Kenyon and Lord Gambier. In 1826, money in hand, Chase bought 8000 acres in Knox County and laid out Kenyon College (originally chartered as a theological seminary) and the town of Gambier.

Chase became the college's first president, a herculean task in the wilderness. He did a fine job, getting the school established, but, by 1831, differences between himself and his clergy prompted him to resign both the Kenyon College presidency and the Episcopate of Ohio. Fortunately, the school survived a change of management, and has continued to flourish since then. It is one of the most respected colleges in the nation, and one of the most beautiful anywhere.

The house sketched here has probably undergone many changes. It is possible that the front portion has been added to an original house in the rear. It was bought several years ago by St. Michael's Catholic Church. An elementary school was built behind the house, and beautiful, new St. Michael's Church, just completed, stands immediately north of the old Episcopal Bishop's home.

Big Horse Business

TWO YOUNG Columbus couples, the Paveys and the Brobsts, lived in houses side by side. When each decided to build, in 1902, they chose a site way out at the north edge of the city and built, side by side, two nearly identical, red brick houses.

Charles William Pavey Sr. was a horse merchant. Back of his new home at 2259 North High, he built a big sales barn where buyers gathered for the Pavey auction each Friday and Saturday. Business grew until Pavey had to build another barn (and eventually three barns) on Lane Avenue, west of the Olentangy. Sales ware attended by 50 to 150 buyers. Many bought entire carloads. The firm commonly sold 500 horses a week, or even as many as 1000 in a single day. At prices averaging $200, that spelled really big business.

Pavey's agents combed Central Ohio for horses which were accumulating in the barns all week. Disastrous sickness was a bugaboo that could wipe out a horse dealer when distemper struck swiftly and fatally. But Bill Pavey was "just about the smartest horse man anywhere." He discovered that horses were far less susceptible to disease if, instead of being tied in stalls, they were left loose in large pens, with no grain but plenty of hay and water. Also, he kept his inventory moving — never keeping a horse over the weekend. His sons, Hugh, Roy and Charles, helped handle horses, and often delivered strings of six to 20 to surrounding towns. Carloads of horses were shipped out of state and to cities as distant as Philadelphia.

When war began in Europe in 1914, tremendous numbers of horses were bought by agents of the allied armies. Pavey sold horses meeting specifications for "seige gun horses" literally by the thousands. He had to use the barns at the Ohio State Fairgrounds. Charles Jr. recalls that his father once sold 180 horses, individually, in three hours — an average of one a minute.

Charles W. Pavey Jr. was born in the house sketched here. He attended Northwood School a few doors south (built in 1878 and still in use), old North High School on Fourth Avenue and the Ohio State University where he completed his medical schooling in 1928. As evidence of the respect his profession has for him, he has been president of both the Columbus Academy of Medicine and the Association of American Physicians and Surgeons.

Several years ago he bought the Brobst home (second in the sketch) and made it his office. About 1940, he began to restore and beautify both the old family home and his office. The completed task has been done so tastefully and handsomely that passersby exclaim about the elegance of this "private urban renewal." Almost the entire block is now beautified and beautifully kept — an example to all the city of what can be done to *keep* itself superlatively attractive without public funds.

County Home

ONCE referred to as "The Infirmary," this building is now called the County Home. It is located on Alum Creek Drive at Frebis Avenue, a short distance south of Livingston.

I had often passed but never stopped to visit until a recent hot (97 degree) Saturday when I drove up the winding roadway to see the County Home close up. It was a surprisingly pleasant haven so I seized the opportunity to sketch in the cool shade of the huge Buckeye trees.

Bill Trayte, clerk of the Franklin County Commissioners and long-time friend, came through nobly when I asked for help on the building's history. Among other things he sought out a huge volume, the "Commissioners' Journal" for 1882. There, preserved in fine copperplate handwriting, were the doings of the board of 83 years ago. Bill noted many references to the then-proposed Infirmary—to make comfortable provisions for the unfortunate poor, is a duty incumbent on all . . ." It was decided that plans should provide for 250 residents. The "cottage plan" was discussed but rejected as not practicable.

By April 10 plans were complete (I found no mention of the architect) and bids were being accepted as follows:

excavating, Jeremiah Cohen, $1080; cut stone work, Mathias Long, $2809; stone masonry, Charles Gutheil, $6800; brickwork, Charles Gutheil, $18,000; wrought iron, Columbus Machine Company, $4423; carpenter work, John Harding, $20,135; tin and galvanized iron work and slating, W. R. Kinnear & Co., $6190.

Richard A. Rowland won the plastering and stucco contract at $4086. Painting and glazing was bid in by Kaiser & Son at $1960. Gas piping was awarded to A. Schwartz at $397. Plumbing, by the same contractor, was at $2795. The entire steam heating contract was awarded to R. Read at $5918. The clerk noted that Commissioner Robinson "protested against allowing any contract to Mr. Read on account of his poor work furnished to the County at the erection of the Children's Home". There was no indication that this was acted upon.

The total cost was to be $74,673.70, an unbelievable figure for the enormous structure. A clue to the low cost is in the board's decision to hire a general superintendent of construction, a very responsible job at, presumably, top wages. The choice for the job was J. E. Hartman. He was to receive three dollars a day for eight months "or until the structure was under roof."

At State and Sixth

I**T WAS** a most unusual house and over the years it had a succession of most unusual tenants. The first, and its builder, was Dr. Francis Carter.

Dr. Carter was born in Ireland and educated at King's College in Dublin. He came to Columbus in 1843 and soon had a large practice. It was his dream to see his adopted city become the medical center of "the West." He persuaded city founder, Lyne Starling (his wife's uncle) to endow such a school. When the gift was made architects were invited to submit designs. The winner was New Yorker Richard A. Sheldon whose Gothic dream (or nightmare, if you choose) dazzled the trustees and bankrupted the school even before it was completed. But its picturesque towers lasted more than a hundred years; were razed to clear the site for present Grant Hospital in 1956.

Dr. Carter, while the school was being built, had Sheldon design this house. It was built across from the school where the Catholic Center now stands. It, too, is Gothic and, like the school, created its own skyline of curious towers and chimneys. Described as a Columbus showplace it was soon mortgaged by the doctor to provide funds for the school. His sacrifices continued as he taught for five years without salary. He apparently had to find cheaper living quarters for his house was leased to the newly elected governor, Salmon P. Chase, in 1855. Chase

and his beautiful, imperious daughter, Kate, made it a dazzling social center during his two terms in office.

Chase was a leading contender for the presidency in 1860. But the first balloting at the Chicago convention of the new Republican party gave him only half as many votes as Lincoln.

In the meantime the Gothic house was bought by Peter Hayden, Columbus' foremost industrialist and financier. His enterprises included three foundries and metal fabricating plants, Haydenville Mining & Manufacturing Company (which owned 3000 acres in Hocking County, mined coal and made a host of clay products) and the Hayden Bank of Columbus.

Sometime about the turn of the century the Knights of Columbus bought and converted the house into their headquarters. Later they built their auditorium at Sixth and Oak. In 1924 they razed the house and built their huge, new club building. A single room of the Carter-Chase-Hayden house still stood, attached to the auditorium.

In 1952 Byer & Bowman Advertising Agency bought and remodeled the auditorium. In the process that last room (said to have been Chase's library) was razed and the agency's private television theater erected on its foundations.

Heilige Kreuz

COLUMBUS' first Catholic church was tiny St. Remigius. (St. Remigius, Archbishop of Rheims, France, died in 533 after a reign of 74 years in the Episcopacy, longest on record.) It was built of rough limestone and stood in the now open corner at lower left in my sketch.

The lot at Fifth and Rich streets had been given to the Dominican Fathers by Otis and Samuel Crosby and Nathaniel Medbery in May, 1833. The gift was conditional — that a church be erected within five years. The Catholics of Columbus were so few in number and poor in purse that they nearly failed to meet the deadline. But, just under the wire, in April, 1838, the little stone church was occupied while still unplastered, unpainted and without seats. Father Henry Damien Juncker sang High Mass, the first ever celebrated in Columbus. In 1843 came Rev. William Schonat, Columbus' first resident priest. Recently from Silesia, he preached in German, most appropriately since most of the congregation understood only that language.

By 1846 a sorely needed larger church was under construction. One C. Jacobs, architect, planned an edifice of brick in the Gothic style with stone foundations and trim, to be built "in substantial fashion with good supporting buttresses." That they did build substantially is proved by the 120 years it has stood. On January 16, 1848 it was dedicated by Bishop Purcell and named "Church of the Holy Cross" which is *Heilige Kreuz* in German.

Father Juncker was succeeded in 1848 by Rev. Casper Henry Borgess, the future Bishop of Detroit, who remained 10 years. During his pastorate the impressive tower and soaring spire were added as well as many interior improvements. In the meantime the little stone church was used as a school; the Sisters of Notre Dame having taken charge of it in 1856. In 1860 the present rectory was built north of the church. And in 1870 the new school was completed, practically as it stands today. The L-shaped structure contained "eight large classrooms and a fine lecture hall." At one end of the building is a tablet bearing the inscription *Heilige Kreuz Schule.*

Holy Cross School continued to operate for more than 100 years. In 1961, with most of its neighborhood of homes razed, it was no longer needed and was closed. I talked to Father Richard Dodd, pastor since 1962. He told me the the building now serves as a Cursillo Center for Christian Renewal classes. He also told me that Holy Cross Church will continue in its present location and mentioned in passing that its massive walls and buttresses contain 800,000 bricks. The leveling of surrounding buildings has revealed the quaint charm of the old quadrangle, nowhere better seen than from my vantage point, the roof of the new 12-story Holiday Inn just west of Holy Cross.

Spy House

BOLD as brass, he was—the handsome young civilian who presented himself at the gates of Camp Chase and demanded admission. Chase, four miles west of the Statehouse, was crammed to the walls with Southern prisoners of war in this latter year of the rebellion.

The brash visitor was told that civilians were rigidly excluded. But he turned on "his wonderful powers of persuasion" insisting he must locate an erring brother (they were supposed to be from Michigan), to deliver a message. At last he was permitted to circle and inspect the camp from the catwalk atop the walls. He didn't locate the mythical brother but what he saw and carefully memorized could come in mighty handy. He was Major Andrew Jackson Marlow of the Confederate Army and he was spying for the South.

Marlow, a native of Virginia, had fought all through the war, until a few weeks before, under Gen. Jubal Early. His courage, charm and resourcefulness brought him the dubious honor of an espionage assignment. Camp Chase was a prime objective since plans were maturing for a general "jail break" at several Northern P.O.W. camps. Accurate details were needed by the planners.

The young Major needed all his talents to travel safely through the undecided areas south of the Ohio and to get across that river. But then he quite casually assumed the Michigan civilian identity and traveled by train to Columbus. Southern prisoners were being marched from the Union Station, out West Broad Street almost daily. To observe these movements Marlow rented quarters in a little brick house at 750 West Broad—the house in my sketch. From its windows he could watch all troop movements in the direction of the prison camp.

Marlow's other northern adventures included a trip to the Wheeling Island prison camp in the Ohio River and a Pittsburgh trip to check on Union defenses. On the latter junket he travelled with a fellow spy who was later unmasked and executed. Marlow was undaunted. His most audacious exploit was to actually recruit 23 Northerners who sympathized with the South, to convoy them to Staunton, Virginia, and there to see them safely inducted into the Confederate Army. Then, after reporting his findings, he returned to Ohio.

He was still busily spying when the war ended. He returned home but found himself attracted to Ohio; moved here and lived many years a few blocks from the little spy house. He died in 1915, at 231 Clarendon Avenue, just 50 years after the war ended. His son, Clifford, still lives in Columbus, at 4085 Hickman Road. The spy house, sketched from a turn-of-the-century photo, was torn down a few years ago.

Clinton Chapel

I WONDER if ever a former church has had as many and varied careers as this one at Walhalla Road and North High Street. Presently it is a striking, handsomely appointed funeral chapel. Owner Robert T. Southwick told me some of its remarkable history then referred me to Clintonville's ablest historian, Mrs. J. Boyd Davis. She filled in the details.

Once it was Clinton Chapel, Methodist and the only church between Columbus and Worthington. The church was organized in 1819 (eight years after Clinton Township was created) by Thomas Bull. It met in various places until 1838 when this structure was built on land given by Bull.

It is little wonder that it has lasted all these years. The foundation walls, of huge glacial boulders, are as much as 56 inches thick. The brick walls of the chapel are 21 inches thick at the base and taper to 16 inches at their tops. The wooden beams are great, adzed logs from the forest, joined by wooden pins. The original roof was of split-oak shingles. The sanctuary was on the second floor, reached by a steep flight of stairs in front. The two dormers, apparently part of the original design, created the desired cruciform plan.

Before the Civil War it served as one of the many local stations on the Underground Railway. The tiny room where escaping slaves were hidden may still be seen.

Then, in 1881, the church was sold for a few hundred dollars and its checkered career began. Sadie Legg has told that her family used it as a home and dairy barn; living upstairs and stabling cows below. Later it was used for farm storage and a horse barn.

Gradually the city crept northward. Farms gave way to wide-spread residences, the old church among them. At one time Columbus' city smoke inspector, Mr. "Smoke" Sullivan bought it, remodeled it into three apartments and lived there. In 1895 Walhalla Road cut through and took part of its yard. For a time, during prohibition, the one-time church was a speakeasy—soon routed by popular demand. It took on its most unusual role as the high-lofted studio of the Armbrusters, painters of stage scenery. It, the Albert Armbruster home next door and a barn all got handsome new roofs of red tile. Their German garden and its wonderful grape arbors stretched clear to California Avenue.

In 1939 Raymond Southwick, Robert's father, bought and further remodeled the building. He added the two-story portico and massive columns. Later additions included the large wing at right. Gleaming stucco over the old bricks (burned on the site) and its commanding position continue to make the 127-year-old structure a north side landmark.

Walk Through History

"TAKING a walk back through history" is not a mere figure of speech if you happen to be in the Center of Science and Industry at 280 East Broad Street. For there, on the second floor, you can do just that, in the Durell Street of Yesteryear.

The street is unique among restorations in that it represents three distinct urban periods — from the 1830s to the early 1900s. Even the pavements are authentic for their periods. The earliest is hardpan clay with wheel tracks and hoofprints; the middle is cobblestone and the latest is patterned paving brick. The corresponding sidewalks are of wood, brick and concrete. Street lighting progresses also, from oil to gas to electricity. The sketch shows a gas lamp on the left and an oil lamp on the right. The overall lighting is planned to simulate deep dusk, making the lighted interiors most effective.

To make my drawing I sat in front of the Dream Land Nickelodeon where silent-screen favorites are shown on weekends. (Its 60-seat auditorium is used for history teaching during the week.) Other, later period businesses include a department store, jewelry store, photo gallery, penny arcade and print shop. I couldn't show them or the general store which is around the corner to the left. The paper mill is yet to be equipped but to its right is the blacksmith shop with complete and authentic equip-

ment. Isaac Norris started it at Orange, Ohio, in 1865. It was in operation until 1963 when it was purchased for the street. Its forge with gigantic bellows is of special interest. Next to it is the harness shop with tools and stitching machines from the old George Zellner Shop in Mansfield.

That this was the horse age is abundantly evident. There's the life-size horse in the blacksmith shop and the silhouette over its door. There's a model horse in the harness shop window and, right across the street, is a horse head hitching post. A real western-style hitching rack edges the wooden sidewalk. Around the corner is a rare, 12-man pumper fire engine, made in 1855 and given by the Nationwide Insurance Company. Other gifts, representative of the different periods, are being sought to complete the interiors of the drug store, department store and photo shop.

The entire street is the creation of Gordon Keith with the Franklin County Historical Society's Daniel Prugh and Edward Durell as consultants. Its cost was borne by the Union Fork and Hoe Company in memory of that company's founder, the late George Britton Durell. The center, with its marvelous models and scientific displays, is open Sundays and holidays 1-5 p.m.; Mondays 1-9 p.m. and Tuesdays through Saturdays 10 a.m.-4:30 p.m.

Roxbury Road

BACK in 1964 I made a Vignette of picturesque old "Casparis Castle" at the southern end of Roxbury Road in Marble Cliff. At the time I had been struck by the beauty of this narrow little almost-country-road of a street. It wanders along the crest of the hill that marks the edge of the village and which once provided spectacular settings for the summer homes of prominent Columbus families. But it wasn't one of the mansions that captured my fancy. It was this low, friendly home with its long, inviting veranda. Huge trees around it bespeak its considerable age yet its lines are as modern as today. The central of its three dormers sports a gambrel roof—unique in my experience. I decided to visit it again.

This spring I went back to 1492 Roxbury (an easy number to remember) to make the sketch I'd mentally composed. And then I asked the home's owner, Robert C. Williams, what he could tell me about it. To my surprise and delight I learned that he had bought it 30 years ago from Bradley Skeele, one of my oldest friends. I found that Brad had moved to Santa Fe, New Mexico, where my hastily written letter reached him and brought these interesting facts by return mail:

"Marble Cliff, originally named 'Arlington,' was laid out in 1889. It was among the first portions of the Miller Farm to be subdivided. (James Turrell Miller, shoe com-

pany founder and street railway tycoon, owned 1000 acres between the rivers. His home still stands as part of First Community Village.)

"Much later, in 1913, more of the farm was sold and *Upper* Arlington was created. Roxbury Road was, at first, plain Central Avenue. The newer name is much more in keeping with its character.

"About the turn of the century there was an Arlington Club just north of our home. Later it became the home of S. P. Bush, president of Buckeye Steel Castings, and the new Arlington Country Club was built a few blocks south. It was just across a ravine from the Casparis place. The Sheldons, Lindbergs and Hosters all built summer homes in the area.

"My dad had our house built about 1896. It was one of the first if not the first one-floor plans in those parts. I was told that 20 carpenters were working on it at one time. (It was a depression year and jobs were scarce.) Frank Packard, leading architect of his day, designed the house. He patterned it after a house he had admired in Switzerland."

Few neighborhoods in the city have remained so delightfully unspoiled for nearly three-quarters of a century. And the house itself is testimony that nice, clean, uncluttered lines are practically timeless.

'Absolutely Fireproof'

A TIDIER little chunk of a building you never saw. Although quite large, its monumental facade dwarfs its doors and creates an illusion of modest size. It is located at 22 West Gay Street.

I was first attracted to the structure by a 1912 newspaper story. Identified as the Rankin Building, it was brand new and praised as "the first absolutely fireproof business and office building in Ohio." The details were impressive: "No wood or other combustible material has been used in its construction. Not a carpenter was employed. Not a nail was driven. Brick and stone walls, bolts, screws and rivets bind it together. All furniture throughout the building is made of metal. The doors and windows are made of iron, and the windows have asbestos shades. Even the stepladders used by the janitors are of galvanized iron. The chairs, tables and desks are all of metal construction. The pictures are framed in metal. The sticks to lower and raise the windows are iron."

L. L. Rankin had purchased the land in 1898. Part of it was occupied by the Munich Building, housing the once-celebrated Kaiserhoff Saloon. The old building became the home of the infant Buckeye State Building & Loan Company. By 1912 Rankin had succeeded to the presidency of the firm and had built this new building. (Fifteen years later the firm built and moved into the present Buckeye Federal Building at 36 East Gay Street, formerly the site of the B. F. Keith Theater of fond memory.)

This building's third floor was once an auditorium, especially attractive for its fireproof quality, called "Rankin Hall." Among interesting facts, the building is surrounded by streets and alleys on all four sides. In front is Gay Street. On the west is Wall Street. Narrow alleys edge it on the east and north. It must be unique for a building this size to be so completely an island unto itself. Still another curious fact emerged as I researched: pictures of the building circa 1912 and 1916 show it with a perfectly plain facade, without columns, archway or bronze doors. The front has obviously been drastically remodeled. Yet no one I contacted had any memory about such remodeling. It is possible that the pictures of the plain-front variety were from architect's renderings; that the building has always had its classic entry. Perhaps some reader will remember and pass along the facts.

Number 22 now serves as the Columbus headquarters for The Kissell Company, principal offices of which are in Springfield, Ohio.

Oak Street Holdout

I'VE ALWAYS admired this honest gray house at 221 Oak Street, just west of Fifth Street. It stands between a tall, old apartment building and a fenced parking lot, looking beleaguered but defiant. It was the home for 78 years of a wonderful lady known to thousands of Columbus school children.

Miss Tallmadge A. Rickey, now almost 90 and living at First Community Village, was a first grader at Lancaster when her father, J. W. Rickey decided to move his family to Columbus. The year was 1885 and his eldest daughter was ready for college. She entered OSU and graduated in 1889. There were just two girls in her class, Alla Berta Rickey and Alberta Garber.

When Mr. Rickey bought this house it was a story-and-a-half cottage, the middle one of three identical homes. He bought it from "Auntie" Thomas, who lived next door, and immediately remodeled it into a two-story as it is today. The three arched windows were once in a gable end facing the street.

A second sister, the late B. Mayes Rickey, went to OSU and then finished school at Dr. Curry's School of Expression and Physical Education in Boston. She was physical education teacher at North High School for many years before retiring in the '40s. Tallmadge got her degree at OSU in 1900. For four years she taught "phys

ed" at nearby Miss Phelps School for Girls. It was, as she remembers, in the former Gwinn home on the southwest corner of Fourth and Broad. After some years of teaching at Troy, Ohio, she came home and became a supervisor in Columbus School Department of Physical Education. Then, from 1934 until 1946 when she, too, retired, she taught her specialty at East High School.

Tallmadge told me what a pleasant neighborhood of homes theirs was. The only non-residence was the "Home for Working Girls" at Oak and Fourth (later the YWCA and still later razed). She organized gym classes that worked out in a wooden building behind the home. Dr. Wheaton lived across Oak. His boy, Bob, Pelatiah Huntington's boys from Broad and John Wilson were constant playmates. They all went to school at old Sullivant on State Street, where the Board of Education building stands.

I made my sketch at high noon on one of those hot July days, seated on a wall inside an auto dealer's car storage building. Then I stepped across the street and knocked on the door of the gray house. A sign announced it as "The City Club." I was kindly admitted and invited to look the house over at my leisure. The most unusual feature is a tightly coiled circular staircase with closed ballustrade—quite unlike any I have ever seen. The fine old holdout house now belongs to William Westwater.

The Kelley House

THIS is the house that *was*—and still *is*, in a highly unrecognizable form. It stood for 124 years at 282 East Broad Street. Since 1961 (when it was razed to clear its site for the Christopher Inn) it has reposed as a pile of stones in Wolfe Park. It now is promised that its numbered stones will be reassembled on the grounds of the new museum near the State Fairgrounds.

Alfred Kelley was a titan of his time. He served 43 years in the Ohio Legislature; commencing as its youngest member, at age 25, in 1814, and retiring in 1857, as its oldest. He was the great dominant force in building Ohio's canal system, under unbelievable difficulties, and below estimate. And he aided in building Ohio's second railroad.

Kelley built this, "the finest example of Greek Revival architecture in Ohio," betwen 1836 and 1838. In the raw young city it was a princely palace. Yet, when Ohio was faced with repudiation of its bonds, he pledged it and all his personal wealth to secure new credit for the state. He died here in 1859. His widow and son continued to own the house until 1906. It was the "Governor's Mansion" when James Campbell occupied it in the 1890s. Most of us remember it as the Catholic "Cathedral School," a role it played for more than half a century.

Kelley got quite a bargain when he bought the land. Totaling 18 acres, it stretched from Fifth Street to Grant Avenue and from Broad to Long. Broad Street frontage was 918 feet—and he bought it all for $917! Even so his purchase was promptly dubbed, "Kelley's Folly." Not only was it considered remote from town, but it was largely a morass, so treacherous that a cow was said to have become mired and sunk from sight close to where the house was built. But stubborn Kelley was a self-made engineer, as well as architect, inventor, lawyer, statesman and entrepreneur. He devised an elaborate drainage system that reclaimed the land. Among its features was a great vaulted tunnel, a "secret passage," that ran from the cellar of the house to at least Fifth Street. Romantics have linked it with the "Underground Railway," but it was probably a mere drainage freeway.

Perfectly symmetrical and severely classical, all four faces of the house had a portico and Greek, Ionic columns. The columns, each a colossal single stone, are said to weigh more than 10,000 pounds apiece. Transporting, handling and erecting such giants was an engineering feat. All the stone was imported, yet the cost of the huge home was only $15,000.

I visited and roamed through it many times in its last years. The very last visit was sickening. Vandals had hacked and slashed and destroyed what little remained of its interior beauty.

Ghost of the 'Big House'

IN 1839 a Baltimore newspaper, trying to make a churlish backwoodsman of Whig candidate, William Henry Harrison, said, "Give him a barrel of hard cider, a pension of two thousand and he will sit the remainder of his days in his log cabin." The jibe backfired. The Whigs made their campaign emblems a log cabin and a keg of cider. "Westerners" from Ohio and beyond went wild with worship of their fellow backwoodsman.

Elected by an enormous majority as a man of humble estate, Harrison was actually a blueblood born in a mansion, Berkeley, in Tidewater Virginia. A wealthy man, William's grandfather married Anne Carter, daughter of "King" Carter, richest man in the Colonies. William's father was governor of Virginia, a signer of the Declaration and officer of the Revolution. William, too, became a soldier, fighting Indians and British from 1791 until 1814 when he retired as a major general.

The house in my sketch is really a ghost. It is supposed to be an authentic replica of the vanished "Big House," the home Harrison built overlooking the Ohio River at North Bend, Ohio. Somewhere inside the original was the log cabin that was laid up when Harrison first settled on his frontier estate. The house grew to mansion size long before the campaign hulabaloo over the log cabin began. (Apparently the Harrisons did live simply; Horace

Mann, after a visit, said, "The whole furniture and ornaments in these rooms might have cost $200 to $225.") Seventeen years after Harrison's death the Big House burned, "set on fire by a she-devil of an Irish woman" said the then occupant.

This replica was built by Ohio for the 1926 world's fair, the Sesquicentennial Celebration in Philadelphia. When the fair closed, the house was dismantled, hauled to Columbus and re-erected on the State Fairgrounds where it still stands. For years it was neglected until a radio personality, Maxine E. Kramer, led a drive to refurbish it. In 1950, with help from the state and "a lot of wonderful companies" it was done over completely—mostly with made-in-Ohio products. Then Maxine and her program, "Eileen Comes Calling," held open house for women's groups, daily for a year and a half.

Since that time the house has had a varied career. It now houses the Herbert Christian Youth Camp. A group of some 60 boys from the Juvenile Diagnostic Center and Fairfield School for Boys live there under the direction of Bill Cummins. He is most enthusiastic over the way his charges help fix up and spruce up various fairground facilities. Even if their pleasant home does contain the ghost of an old log cabin, it is highly unlikely that hard cider is ever on their menu.

On Irish Broadway

IRISH immigrants at mid-19th century tended to cluster around the railroad station and yards at the northern end of Columbus. The dirt road that later became Naghten Street was known as "Irish Broadway." Thus, it was fitting that the first English-language Catholic church was built by the Irish at the head of their "Broadway," at Seventh Street (now Grant Avenue).

The Irish first attended older Holy Cross' German services. Then a second congregation was formed which worshipped there in English at non-conflicting hours. In 1852 they bought their big lot and, on September 5 of that year, laid the cornerstone for this church, 110-year-old St. Patrick's. Ever since that time Irish Catholics of the city have thought of "St. Pat's" as their very own. Many of its pastors have been Irish (Fitzgerald, Gallegher, Delaney, Costello and McKenna). Although many have not (Rosecrans, Larpenteur, Baeszler), each cherished the Irish and bore with patience the temperament of his "wild Irish rogues." Today's pastor, Father John Jordan Reichert, is no exception. He calls himself "the Bavarian Irishman" and no greater devotee of Ireland and things Irish could be found.

With shifting population St. Patrick's finds itself today, with only 15 Catholics in its parish. But a recent tally showed an average Sunday attendance at Mass of 1300. An awful lot of people are crossing parish lines to wor-

ship here. When I told my colleague, Martha Sullivan, that I'd like to do St. Patrick's, her eyes sparkled and she exclaimed, "I *love* that church!" She's proved it by coming clear across town every Sunday, rain or shine, for years. She told me that many come 15 to 20 miles regularly—passing dozens of other churches on the way.

St. Patrick's pastors have included three who later wore the Bishop's Mitre. Four of her Dominican Priests have borne the title "Right Reverend Provincial." Dominicans have cared for the parish since 1885. The school was established in 1854. It reached a peak enrollment of 550 students in grade and high school in 1891, and was closed in 1959 after 105 years of service.

On May 28, 1935, a workman's torch fired the roof. Before it was quenched the fire destroyed nearly all but the walls. But it was rebuilt and restored within a year, including new pews with carved shamrocks. The interior, belying its plain outside, is gorgeous; especially its white, Gothic altar. Rich stained glass, sacred statuary and paintings make it a real gem among churches.

I chose this rather homely view because it shows the church, part of the old school at right and the residence and its quaint dormers and Eastlake porch. The Naghten Street side, by contrast, is clothed in the heavy green of strong, young trees—symbolic, perhaps, of the vigor of Old St. Patrick's itself.

The Village in the City

AMERICANS have been laughed at for trying to create "instant antiquity" by copying Europe's centuries' old architecture. The derision is deserved when a street results that is a potpourri of styles bearing no relationship to each other. One man felt strongly about the unhappy results. The passion for copying was at its height in the 1920s when he conceived a whole village in variations of the Norman French style. Fortunately, he was able to see it realized in what came to be known as Sessions Village.

The land, along the north side of East Broad east of Alum Creek, was part of a huge plot once owned by Francis Sessions. The architect with a vision was Robert R. "Roy" Reeves of the firm Miller & Reeves. He had entered a contest to design an important monument, had won it and his first trip to France. During that and subsequent visits he fell in love with what he described as "the minor domestic architecture of France."

In 1927, a corporation was formed to build the Village. Members were D. W. Fulton, Webb I. Vorys and J. M. Rankin. It was their happy decision to give Roy Reeves *carte blanche*. He proved worthy of their trust. The entire village was planned along two narrow, old-world streets with houses flush with the sidewalks. Walled courtyards and gardens gave privacy and isolated each menage from its neighbors and the surrounding city. Stucco, half-timber, brick, stone, slate and wrought iron were used to the best possible effect. High, pitched roofs and picturesque chimneys, diamond paned windows and a hundred varied and delightful details gave unique character. The winding streets simulated water-bound macadam. The gutters are of granite block and the sidewalks are limestone slabs. Lush planting and wandering ivy soften every angle. The planting and gardens were planned by Carl Frye.

Thirteen houses were built, including the pair of doubles that flank the entrance shown in my sketch. Drawn from just inside the Village it shows the "bridge room" originally accessible only from the enclosed stairway at left. It is said to have been intended for a gateman's lodge, a luxury the depression wiped out. I painted this same view more than 30 years ago and had never gone back until now. Time had done wonderful things that time alone can do. The effect today is truly that of an ancient, albeit marvelously cared-for street abroad. Today there are 14 additional houses, all in the spirit of the originals, designed by Bob Reeves, son of the original architect, Tom Tully, Al Friday and George Crumley. George, whose home is one of the most recently built, is secretary-treasurer of the Village Association. And Mrs. Crumley allowed me to excerpt many of these facts from a paper which she had written concerning this "Village-in-the-City."

43

Blendon's Oldest

WORTHINGTON was still a crude pioneer village in 1806 when two Connecticut families came by ox wagon to settle nearby. Their closest neighbors were in the village nearly five miles to the west. Edward Phelps came with his wife and six children. Isaac Griswold had his wife and two children. Their farms were originally part of a huge parcel of 4000 acres deeded in 1800 by President John Adams to one John Stiles. Stiles probably never visited his baronial holdings, known as Range 17, Township 2, Quarter Township 3. Within four months he had sold it to Matthias Williamson for $1120—less than 30 cents an acre. Then, Aaron Ogden, the next owner, began selling off portions of the property.

Edward Phelps bought 500 acres for $787.50. Griswold took 200 acres adjoining. It was a choice location, astride the Worthington-Granville Road, now Route 161. Phelps first built a cabin north of the road. In 1823, with much of his fine land (overlooking Alum Creek Valley) cleared and in production, he built this big, comfortable New England farmhouse south of the road. There, little changed, it stands today after 143 years. Mrs. L. Francis (Phelps) Wolls is Edward's great granddaughter. She says it is recognized as the oldest house in Blendon Township; yet, it is seldom noticed by motorists passing within a few feet of its front door.

Edward Phelps died in 1840, leaving to his sons, William and Homer, "the farm on which I live and one third of my sawmill." The land had already been divided, for he left "70 acres on which he lives to my son, Edward Phelps Jr." His married daughter, Cloe Gillespie, got 100 acres. Unmarried Azubah got the mixed bag—"100 acres, 2 beds and bedding, $100, the use of my East Room and East Chamber and 2 cows."

I visited the house (at 3047 Granville Road), sketched it and then talked to its present owners, young, gracious James and Margene Harper. They bought it four years ago to give their four children plenty of room. They let me ramble from basement to attic. Both those areas revealed the home's massive framework—of timbers as large as 12 inches square, hand hewn and hard as rock. Big wooden pins held it together. Throughout the house, window and door frames are of a design I'd never seen. Side pieces taper from bottom to top and the lintelboard is a miniature pediment—a vaguely Egyptian motif. The design is abundantly evident since there are 25 doors and 35 windows.

The long wing at the rear includes a smokehouse with a gigantic fireplace and a ceiling still studded with big meathooks. Beyond it is the old carriage house, its framing timbers exposed. I cheated a little on the drawing by arbitrarily removing and rearranging trees which hide most of the house from view.

On Broadway

BOARDED up for years, its lot wildly overgrown, this ghostly gray mansion at Indianola and North Broadway interests a host of people. Nearly 50 have asked that it be the subject of a Vignette. My first casual queries elicited, "It was the Daniel house; Mr. Daniel was a banker." When I learned it is to be razed soon, I dug deeper. Mr. Daniel, I found was not a banker; he was an expert on railroad tariffs and was at times general agent for the Columbus & Eastern and the Columbus, Shawnee & Hocking Railroads.

North Broadway was laid out and the Daniel house built about 1890. Mrs. Leah DeVault believes that the Acton family built it (it was long called "Acton Place"). Mrs. Hazen Rhodes and her brother, Howard Wentz, have a photo showing the Daniel house in a vast expanse of open country. In the distance, at the end of Broadway, was a railroad station, identified as Evanston. A post office of the same name served that once far-north location.

In 1896 the Daniels bought the house from E. Howard Gilkey who had risen from a Civil War-orphaned boy to be law librarian and marshal of Ohio's Supreme Court and, later, a Christian Science practitioner and teacher. The house remained in the Daniel family until 1961, when the last surviving son, Bering, died. The senior Daniels died in the 1930's.

Mary E. Garner told me something of Bering's life.

As a youngster he went into the fascinating automobile business with his older brother, Thomas. The Daniel Motor Car Company at 363 North High is listed in a 1915 directory as "Distributors of New Era Motor Cars and Stewart Delivery Trucks and Pleasure Cars." They hadn't picked winners, it seems, for both soon took jobs. Both went into service during World War I. Thomas went to California. Bering remained with his parents and became a clerk in the Columbus Sewerage and Drainage department, his life-long job. He was often kidded about being B. B. Daniel, namesake of the silent movie star, Beebe Daniels.

The senior Daniels entertained freely and graciously in the early years of the century; kept the house in show-place condition. The 1912 Dau Bluebook says that Ida (Burrows) Daniel "receives on Fridays." She was most active in the affairs of St. Paul's and St. James Episcopal Churches. Many recall their beautiful yard (a full acre) with its flowers and fruit trees. On my last visit I found it a jungle. In spite of a sinister sign, "No Trespassing, Survivors Will Be Prosecuted," I went in at an open window. It was a sad sight. To the ravages of time had been added the ravages of young savages who had smashed and burned and covered every inch of wall space with some exceedingly racy inscriptions. Perhaps it's as well that it will be razed and its ignominy ended soon.

Deshler-Lilley House

JOHN G. DESHLER was scion of a rich banking family. In 1875 he married Minnie Greene, daughter of equally rich Milbury Greene, railroad magnate and also a banker. His father, William G. Deshler, gave them, as a wedding gift, this house at 485 East Broad Street. It was big and elegant, even though its style was just a bit passe for '75. That wasn't what upset the new Mrs. Deshler, however. She complained that "It's just too far out in the country."

It those days Third Street opposite the Statehouse was called "the gold coast" for its row of great town houses. One of them was owned by John W. Lilley and his wife, the former Rachel Cloud. A partner in the hugely successful Siebert & Lilley, bookbinders, John was tired of mid-city living. In 1879 he dickered and finally traded houses with the Deshlers. His daughter, Mrs. George Robinson (Mabel Lilley) and Mrs. Alice Lilley Burns were born at 485. They remember the trade; how it included the carpeting in both houses, some of the servants and John Deshler's fine milch cow.

The Lilleys, good Presbyterians, had been the first couple wed in old Central Presbyterian Church in 1860. But they soon had a Methodist neighbor. Broad Street Methodist Church, the west wall of which is suggested in my sketch, was dedicated in 1885. Thereafter, a Presbyterian cow was often seen cropping Methodist grass.

Mrs. Robinson, her nephew, Howard Wentz and niece, Mrs. Hazen Rhodes, have recalled details of the grand old house, called in a newspaper story, "the showplace of the city, where the nation's most prominent people have been entertained." Its double doors opened into a reception hall with a wide, curving stairway. To the left, in order, were: the ornate parlor, the library, the sitting room, first kitchen, dining room and second kitchen. The woodwork was black walnut. Elaborate chandeliers were of solid bronze. Upstairs were six bedrooms. The third floor was all open and the Lilley sons mounted from it, by ladder, to the rooftop "widow's walk." Out back in the stables were the cow, horses, carriage, buggy and sleigh. East Broad was the favorite street for young bloods racing their cutters when the snow came.

The Siebert & Lilley firm occupied the third floor of the huge Comstock Opera House Building on the west side of High between Rich and Town. In 1892 Columbus' greatest fire to date destroyed the building and all contents.

Mr. Lilley retired but an employe and Judge Gale reorganized under the name Ruggle & Gale, later the Columbus Blank Book Company, a firm still in business. John Lilley died in 1901. Rachel Lilley remained in the house until 1908. She lived until 1942—her 99th year. The house was razed in 1931.

College of Art

SLUMBERING art in Columbus awoke with a bang in 1878. Leading women of the burgeoning city met at the Kelley mansion on East Broad and formed the Columbus Art Association. Its prime concern was to establish a school of art.

That same year, art conscious men met and formed the Gallery of Fine Arts. The ladies, as usual, got more action. In January, 1879, they opened their school in a third-floor room at 15 East Long. Courses at first ran to the feminine (art needlework, china painting and ecclesiastical embroidery) but soon broadened to include drawing of plaster cast models, live clothed-figure models and sculpture. Nudes were still considered too nasty for Columbus. Then began a series of moves.

The first was to Gay and 4th Streets, in the Tuller Building, where the Masonic Temple now stands. It was there that Oscar Wilde visited and complimented it, but said, "It would be better with gardens about . . . instead of plows and reapers and ding-dong of shops." The school's director from 1882 until 1910 was John E. Hussey. He is still going strong, a hale and active 102, living with his daughter, Mrs. H. H. Mock. Equally durable is Mary F. Sweyer, who was a student of his in the 1880s. She is a famous Lancaster artist and close friend of mine, now in her 100th year.

In 1893 the art school moved to the brand new YMCA Building that was located on South 3rd where the *Dispatch* Building stands. Later the school moved to an old residence at 187 East Broad and still later, in 1920, to the former Monypenny home at Broad and Washington. There, as that roaring decade ended, I attended evening classes up under its great mansard roof. Already a fancier of decaying mansions, I was especially fond of the place.

In 1930 the art school got its own handsome home, the building in my drawing, just north of the gallery at the west end of Hutton Place. Strangers must wonder at the complete absence of windows in the two south wings. The principal windows, as most artists prefer, face north.

Because of war and other complications, the school drifted to the edge of oblivion by 1952, when Joseph V. Canzani became director. It had only 13 day students and a faculty of "one and a half." Then it started the climb back up. It had grown considerably by 1959, when it became the Columbus College of Art and Design. Presently it has more than 850 students (full and part time) and a faculty of 45. The main building has long since been outgrown and the school has spilled over into six small, adjacent buildings, plus use of a large part of the gallery.

Tiny Hutton Place is well worth a Sunday afternoon visit, especially to see the little "sculpture courtyard" between two converted residences belonging to the school.

Canal Town's R.R. Station

THE PEOPLE of land-locked interior Ohio contemplated the coming of the canal with joy and thanksgiving. That is, most of them did.

One of the few who took a dim view was Henry Dove, first settler on the site of Winchester. He had arrived in 1802 and had a fine farm when, a quarter century later, the canal was surveyed through it. Mr. Dove, whom I imagine to have been a stern, self-made individualist, objected. He had a fine crop of wheat in the field that was certain to be destroyed by the construction. He threatened to bring suit against the state. Then some canal enthusiast suggested a more profitable move—to lay out a town along the canal and sell lots. Dove followed the suggestion, platting 25 quarter-acre lots along two streets, High and Columbus. He called it Winchester after his ancestral seat in Virginia.

The town flourished. As the center of one of the best grain growing areas in the state, it became a bustling shipping center. In season every street and lane in town was filled with loaded grain wagons. A large lot where High Street crossed the canal was dredged for a boat basin and soon huge grain warehouses sprouted around it. Colorful canal men and grain farmers mingled there, profitably if not always peaceably.

In 1841 the town was to get its first post office and a decision had to be made. Since there were five other Winchesters in Ohio, a new name was needed. Suggestions included Waterloo, Carlisle and Pekin, but the townsfolk chose the old name with an appropriate prefix and it became Canal Winchester.

Although a "Hocking Valley Railroad" was the subject of a resolution in Congress in 1834 (two years before there was a mile of railroad in Ohio) actuality was far off. The first trains ran on the Columbus & Hocking Valley in 1869. As a public relations gesture the line offered a free ride (and a free lunch) from Lancaster to Columbus and return. The result was pandemonium as 1800 passengers jammed into 18 coaches and box cars. At a point just north of the Canal Winchester station in our sketch the laboring locomotive stalled. The free-loaders unloaded themselves, pushed the train with a will and soon were able to all-aboard for Columbus.

The Old Hocking Valley was largely Columbus owned. It made many fortunes in town, hauling Southern Ohio coal. Through merger (and alleged skulduggery) it became the Columbus, Hocking Valley & Toledo in 1880. Fifty years later it became a division of the Chesapeake & Ohio as it is today.

From C&O Assistant Trainmaster E. E. VonSchriltz I learned that the station was built in 1895. There was no known duplicate, although it is instantly recognized as one variation on a theme someone has called "Railroad Gothic." Still in active duty, it is the only remaining station between Columbus and Lancaster.

Canal Tavern

THIS OLD tavern at Lockbourne is one of the remaining relics of Ohio's boldest public work, the Ohio Canal system. It took courage for a new, poor and thinly settled state to plan and complete so gigantic a project. The Ohio-Erie Canal was begun near Newark in 1825 and completed in 1831. Columbus was bitterly disappointed to be off the surveyed route. A branch canal, the "Columbus Feeder," was dug to meet the main canal 11 miles southeast of the city.

Worthington's Colonel James Kilbourne, with Joel Buttles and Demas Adams, foresaw a brilliant future for a town at the junction point of the Columbus Feeder. In 1831 they bought considerable acreage at the point, laid out a town and called it Lockbourne (for the eight nearby locks plus part of the colonel's name). The town flourished while the canal was busy. In 1837 a post office was established and in 1839 William Monypeny built a large distillery. This tavern was erected in 1852 by Josiah Hulva. It stands high above what was the spacious canal boat basin. Hulva was a dedicated Mason and was chief organizer of Lockbourne Lodge No. 232, F. and A. M. Over the door of his tavern is fixed a white marble keystone with the date 1852 and the Masonic Order date, 5852 A. L.

I had a long talk with James Ray who remembers the old canal in action. He came to Lockbourne in 1897 when he was eight. One of his recollections concerns a Clelland family whose permanent home was their freight boat, *Cashier*. Charles and Rhoda Clelland, who started their wedded life on the boat in 1884, spent most of it afloat on the Feeder, hauling hay to supply Columbus Fire Department horses.

Mr. Ray recalls the night Wilbur Clelland was born on the boat while it was anchored in the basin. "Old Doc" H. C. Blake, who was deathly afraid of water, couldn't be coaxed into a rowboat to preside. Young Jim Ray drove a spring wagon pell-mell to Shadeville and got Dr. E. A. Thrall who braved the boat ride to attend Mrs. Clelland. All six of her children were born on the boat, each at a different port.

Mr. Ray, who worked more than 55 years as a Lockbourne blacksmith, remembers the decline of the canal. He believes the feeder was practically abandoned by 1905.

The old tavern, of "five over four design" (five windows above and four below), changed hands many times. It continued as a place of public entertainment until comparatively recent times. Its last public life was as Jimmie Turton's Saloon. Now it is owned by Harless Lozier and serves as a two-family dwelling. Out front is another reminder of pioneer times—half a huge millstone which serves as a carriage step.

Oldest and Largest

NOT LONG ago the Worthington Presbyterian Church found itself 11 years older than had been thought. For years its founding date was considered to be 1816. But research by Mary Alice Stein has proved that it was organized in 1805. Thus it has long since passed its 150th birthday and is the oldest Presbyterian Church in Franklin County.

The little congregation met for some years in various places—private homes, the old Academy, Goble's blacksmith shop and the Masonic Temple. Then, in 1829, Congregationalist-turned-Episcopalian, James Kilbourne, sold his lot at the northeast corner of the Village Green to the congregation for $40. A contemporary report, attributed to a Methodist, was that "The Presbyterians are building a house which is small and plain without any steeple and looks like a barn." Even so, its cost may have been more than the handful of hopefuls could swing, for tradition has it that their first pastor, Rev. Highland Hulburd, journeyed all the way to Philadelphia where he got needed funds from the church's general assembly. The poor little church had to wait a dozen years before it got a steeple and certain other embellishments.

Among its pastors have been famous James Hoge, "father of Presbyterianism" in Franklin County, and Thomas Woodrow, grandfather of President Woodrow

Wilson. Rev. Woodrow's salary, incidentally, was $350 a year in the 1850s. Another presidential connection: the Misses Marjorie and Jessie Wilson, members since 1913, are great-great granddaughters of President John Quincy Adams.

During the early 1920s the church became moribund until Dr. Edward Milton Page became pastor and revitalized it. Through his efforts money was raised for a new church which was dedicated in 1927. Today's handsome columned portico, tower and spire were built at that time. Their beauty of proportion and detail have been praised as equal to any in America. Young Boyd G. Martin, while still a student at Carnegie Tech, designed it, as a member of the firm Martin, Orr & Martin. They also built the church, at a cost of $48,000. The old 1829 church was incorporated in the new structure. (It survived until 1958, when it was torn away during remodeling. The remodeling and enlargement cost $275,741.) The increased size was sorely needed inasmuch as the church grew in 15 years from 603 to 2100 members. Its pastor during this period of growth (since 1950, longest tenure of any of its pastors) has been Paul W. Johnston, D.D. He has seen the little village church literally explode with Worthington's population explosion until it is Franklin County's and Central Ohio's largest Presbyterian Church.

Garden Club Project

WAY BACK in 1924, Columbus area's first garden club was formed. Called Franklin Garden Club, its only concern was members' own gardens. Then, in 1940, it took on its first public service task — supplying and caring for plants in the courtyard of the Columbus Gallery of Fine Arts. It was rewarding work since plants thrived in the then-open, sunny yard.

Then two problems developed: The Gallery, pressed for more space, eyed the vast courtyard covetously. And, about the same time, the courtyard floor began to leak into storage rooms below. The solution to both was to roof over the expanse, a project completed in 1953 with funds provided by Mrs. Lillie Gill Derby. The newly-created room was named "Derby Court."

But solving one set of problems introduced others. The plants and flowers that once grew so nicely "took to their beds," figuratively, after being taken from beds and put into pots. Franklin members studied, experimented, selected, planted, transplanted and nursed the kinds of greenery needed to soften the harshness of the big, bare room and provide settings for sculpture. The big pots, irresistible to smokers, ended up as gigantic ashtrays and unofficial refuse receptacles. Art School students, when they paint in the court, find the pots a handy place to dispose of paints, turpentine and other non-recommended plant food. The room is much used for big-crowd functions, so the plants are often shuffled about; even moved outside where, once, a number of them froze. And the hot sun pouring through the great coffered skylights was such a hazard that the club had to install plastic light filters. The battle still goes on, with the good guys winning most of the time.

The Franklin Club has had flower shows at the Gallery for 25 years, inducing many to visit it for the first time. Leafing through Franklin's yearbooks for that quarter century, I note that special credit for devoted service is due artist-gardeners Mark and Mary Russell and Mary Louise Harrison. At this very moment there is a big flower extravaganza at the Gallery. Titled "Christmas Contrasts," it is open today from noon until 4 p.m. Franklin is one of the 29 participating clubs in the Columbus Council of Garden Clubs of Ohio staging the event.

My sketch of a corner of the courtyard shows how plants are used to set off sculpture. The figure is the work of Columbus' famous Erwin F. Frey. Interestingly, the marble was twice torn violently from its environment before Frey took chisel to it. First it was blasted from a southern quarry; then it was blasted from the walls of the Ohio State Office Building by an explosion that shattered the building in 1930. Frey got it as salvage.

Another 'Folly'

HOWARD E. WENTZ, who often has helped me with stories, mentioned "Jacobs' Folly" the other day and got my immediate interest. I'd heard of Kelley's, Swayne's and Fritter's Follies, but this was a new one. When he described it as a huge octagon house at 450 East Norwich, I remembered Johnny Jones once mentioning it and suggesting I investigate it. With Howard's help I pieced out the story.

Felix A. Jacobs was born in Columbus in 1840. His German immigrant father was a gunsmith. Felix and two brothers apparently inherited his mechanical ability. As youths they began making agricultural implements. In 1881 they helped to found famous Kilbourne & Jacobs Manufacturing Company, which sold its wrought steel products all over the world. The company prospered and the Jacobs family grew rich.

Felix, his brother, William and sister, Bertha lived in a great, gray mansion on Hamlet Street not far from the plant. The three, all single, lived austerely, acquiring a neighborhood reputation as eccentric millionaires. Felix's eccentricity seemed proved when he began to build this house in the early 1920s. I was told that he first sought a city building permit for his "ideal home" and was refused because he had no plans and that he therefore built on this site because at that time it was still outside the city. Whatever the truth, he did do a lot of improvising and personally supervised the pouring of the thousands of tons of concrete that went into his fortress-like, 18-inch-thick walls. Octagon houses were not new, but his was decidedly novel. For instance, it was entirely air conditioned—first in the city; perhaps the first anywhere. All the original windows were solid and fixed in place. As he designed it, the house was one story with a concrete roof. His intention was to create a sort of Babylonish hanging garden on it, with trees, shrubs and flowers growing in thick turf. Thus his living quarters would be a cool, "above ground, under ground." They were divided into eight big pie-shaped rooms with a mechanical core at the center. In it, in a shallow pit, was the gas heating and cooling system. The floor is a solid concrete slab except for a tunnel running underneath. It, and a well of cold water, were part of the cooling system. The curious central stack was supposed to help, but the system never worked. As it turned out, nothing worked very well. The concrete walls sweat excessively; the concrete roof leaked and heating costs were enormous. After spending some $40,000, Felix gave up on it and the house stood empty for years.

About 1937 Glenn I. Hay, a WPA official, bought it for $4500. He added the second story and divided it into apartments as it is today. Felix is said to have lived a hundred years. And Howard Wentz says the house might well last twice that—that the only more solid affair hereabouts is Ohio Stadium.

Beloved Briarfield

BRIARFIELD, at 6020 Havens Corners Road, is in good hands. Dr. and Mrs. Robert L. Stratton, who have owned it just a year, cherish it as deeply as its previous owner, Wayne A. Stallman, who gave it its name after the home of his grandmother's cousin, Confederate President Jefferson Davis. Stallman spent 15 years of hard work and a lot of money restoring it to perfection.

It was built in 1837 by Isaac Souder who bought the original 224 acres from William Stanberry for $674. He and his bride had come from Virginia with high hopes and little money. At first they built a tiny cabin whose foundation stones still remain. Then, as their family grew and they prospered, they planned an elegant home. Isaac returned to Virginia, sought and admired anew the model he intended to duplicate. He had an artist make careful drawings; brought them and several fine craftsmen back to Ohio with him.

Just east of Briarfield is a tiny lake. It was created as clay was dug there to make bricks. They were burned a few yards in front of the house site and building was begun. The main structure had (and has) four huge rooms and generous hallways on its two floors. At the back is the big living-kitchen and beyond it the smaller "keeping room." Every room has a fireplace. The one in the kitchen is huge, with the original wrought iron cooking crane still in place. It was lined with "bog ore" to resist heat. The

house was built for the ages with walls a foot and a half thick. No sign of a crack has ever appeared.

Isaac lived 43 years in his fine home. When he died it went to his daughter, Eliza Ealy. She died in 1918 and her son, the late Simon Ealy inherited it. Mrs. Ethel Ealy lived there 30 years, selling it to Stallman in 1951. The Stallmans wanted it as a setting for their beautiful antiques, and a more fitting one can't be imagined. All of their work was true restoration—preserving every sound piece of wood or replacing it with a perfect duplicate. The only exterior additions were the "burglar bars," lacy cast-iron filigree work at the base of each window. Stallman had them cast from originals. The classic Greek Revival carriage porch was so out of repair that it was carefully measured and duplicated in new wood. Wavy, handmade glass was carefully fitted into new wood around the front entrance.

The Strattons visited the house a few years ago, loved and coveted it. When Stallman decided to sell he chose them to have it because he knew how they felt about it. Their handsome antiques (most of which were refinished by Mary Ellen Stratton) look as though they had been in the house for all its 129 years. The Strattons are doing all of their redecorating in authentic Federal style. The house, I'm sure, has never looked more beautiful and more worthy of being so lovingly preserved.

'Society House'

NO ONE would call this a distinguished house. If one had to give its style a name, "Middle American Mongrel" would do as well as any. Originally it was a double, numbers 499 and 503 Oak Street, at Washington. Lewis Huffman, maker of wooden pumps (bored out lengths of 6x6 pine that served as pump, pipe and all) bought the lot in 1869. It is more than likely that he bought it in anticipation of coming transportation. It came, in 1872, in the form of the State & Oak Street Railroad, a horsecar line running from State and High to East Public Lane, now Parsons Avenue. He built this commodious house of eight rooms a side as an investment. On a carline, it rented easily and steadily. Dozens of families called it home over several years. In 1920, Huffman's daughter, Ida, sold the house and the distinguished part of its history began.

The purchaser, the non-profit Columbus TB Society, then in its 14th year, thus acquired its first permanent home. The Society had begun as a committee of the Instructive District Nurses Association. By 1906, it was on its own as the Columbus Society for Prevention and Cure of Tuberculosis. Mrs. Samuel L. Black was elected president, a job she was to hold for 30 years. At once the Society sought to set up a free clinic and dispensary. The disease was so dreaded that most doors were hysterically closed and quarters were very hard to find. It wasn't a

senseless fear for in that year one death in six was from TB. The dispensary was finally opened. Much of its staff and its medical director served without salary.

The Society did much direct work but also sought in every way to educate both the public and officials of city schools. It was agreed that tuberculous children should have a separate school. A first attempt to locate it north aroused a furor. A petition backed by the North Side Chamber of Commerce blocked it. A second location was acquired on the West Side. It also raised a storm of protest, so violent that the city bought the land from the Society and made it a park. At last, in 1913, the School Board provided a site at Hudson and Neil and a school was opened. Pressure on the county resulted in the first TB Sanitarium, near the County Infirmary, in 1914.

The famous TB Christmas Seal Sale was, for years, a small affair, raising less than $2000. In 1919, its 10th year, the sale was sponsored by the Columbus Rotary Club and raised an astonishing $59,000. Part of the money was used to buy this house. This year's sales goal is $225,000 which will support a tremendous program of education, detection and research on TB and other pulmonary diseases. Last month, 46 years to the day after the Society moved into the old house, it moved out and into a new, snug and functional building of its own at 185 South Fifth Street.

1899 Pleasure Palace

"NO DAINTY bit of Venetian art surpasses the beauty of this wonderful combination of towers, turrets and pinnacles." Thus, did a prideful press agent for the Dusenbury Brothers liken a Columbus structure to architecture in the "Jewel of the Adriatic." He was writing in 1899, as the decade forever to be known as "Gay" was coming to a close. Location of the "structure" was then "way up north," on the west side of High Street above Arcadia. It was called Olentangy Park Theater.

Back in the 1880s Robert M. Turner built a tavern on the site and called it Olentangy Villa because of the nearby river. In 1895 it was taken over by the thriving Columbus Railway, Power & Light Company which added picnic grounds and some facilities for amusement, including gambling. (Those were the days when street railway and interurban firms were generating traffic, as well as electricity, and developing edge-of-city amusement parks.) In 1899 the Dusenburys acquired and greatly expanded the park. They installed a swimming pool, restaurant, bowling alleys and rental boat docks on the river. And they built this gaudy structure, billed as "the largest and finest summer theater in America."

As a further sample of their press agent's work, behold; "The great building stands on the high bank of the river, 56 feet above the water and will be the crowning glory of the most beautiful spot around Columbus . . .

when completed will prove a delightful bewilderment of piazzas and promenades, belfries, balconies, turrets and terraces, corners and cozy nooks. It will seat 2248 in elegant opera chairs . . . illuminated by nearly 2000 electric lamps. The orchestra pit, which is the largest in Columbus, is for Neddermeyer's Orchestra of 15 pieces. This superb musical organization will also give daily concerts in the bandstand overlooking the river." Most astonishing to us, today, "The imposing structure represents an outlay of over $25,000."

A summer theater of this size could flourish in Columbus because the big, Downtown theaters offering stage fare closed during the hottest months. Summer theaters, designed to catch every breeze, were air-conditioned by nature. They offered stock company drama and vaudeville and their patronage was enormous.

I found the picture upon which I based my drawing in an 1899 magazine. I suspect the original artist of adding a few touches to please the Dusenburys. Certainly by my time it was much simpler; it had been stripped of its frills as they decayed, and the great "piazzas and promenades" were gone.

Everything is gone now—nearly 100 acres of amusements: theater, ballroom, rides of every description and all. In their place, since 1937, has been the handsome apartment community, Olentangy Village.

The Brevoort Place

IT IS PERFECTLY possible to pass this brick cottage for dozens of years without noticing it. I've proved it by doing just that. It seems incredible now that I've learned that the site and house wrap up a lion's share of Clintonville Township's early history; or perhaps I should say, "Bull's share."

Thomas Bull, a native of Vermont, came to Worthington in 1812 with four stout sons and one of his two daughters. He bought 600 acres of land comprising most of present Clintonville. Soon after, his second daughter, Chloe, arrived with her husband, Isaac Brevoort and son, Henry. They built a log cabin near Bull's land along the Worthington Road. There another son, Jason, was born. Then tragedy struck.

Isaac was helping build a barn across the Whetstone River. He was crossing the flood-swollen stream in February, 1814 when his boat was swamped and he was drowned —one of the first of many victims of the Whetstone (Olentangy) at flood tide.

Henry Brevoort stayed on the land and, in 1850, built this snug brick home just back of the old cabin (stones still mark the cabin site) at 3620 North High Street. Three generations of Brevoorts have lived in it during its 116 years. Frank, who died last summer at 90,

lived there nearly 80 years. Most of the 100-acre farm was sold long ago. Eighty acres of it were sold for what seemed the large sum of $8000. But Pegg Realty paid $82,000 for the same piece in the early 1920s. It is now the Northmoor section, according to Joe Landon, himself a realtor and a grandson of old Henry.

Joe told me that his mother inherited half the remaining 20 acres; that she sold it in 1908 to Thompson, Johnson & Thompson who developed Brevoort Road. This old house finally remained on a plot of something over an acre. Mrs. John Caronis, who lives next to it on Brevoort, says that Frank kept his little estate as one of the most charming spots in Columbus. Giant locust trees, planted more than 100 years ago, flourish as do dozens of younger trees and evergreens. Once past the pair of fieldstone gateposts, one is hardly aware of the surrounding city. The ancient barn where Frank once operated a dairy still stands. He had flower beds, pools for lilies and giant gold fish, fruit trees and berry bushes and, while he was still able, a generous garden. "He was always busy," Mrs. Caronis said, "even painted his house when he was past 80." Most amazing, he painted the bricks and then outlined each one in black while perched precariously on a tall stepladder, she remembers.

'The Gingerbread House'

MANY PEOPLE have told me that they "just love this "Gingerbread House." I do too; but none of us could love it as do the wonderful couple to whom it has been home for 48 years. Mark and Mary Russell moved into their home at 5807 North High Street in 1919, just about the time Mark started to teach at Columbus Art School.

He had already had a considerable career as an artist. His schooling at the Art Students League in New York had been sandwiched between stints as a designer for the Von Gerichten Art Glass Company. There he created many notable windows for churches including widely separated Broad Street Presbyterian in Columbus and the Church of the Tranfiguration in New York (famous as "The Little Church Around the Corner"). In the meantime he was developing a fabulous decorative pen style that led him to the top in his field. Edna M. Clark, art historian, calls him "one of the finest designers in the country." Mary goes a step further, calmly asserting, "He is *the* finest."

After some time spent freelancing, doing decorative newspaper pages for a syndicate and book illustration, he began to teach. In addition to the Art School (where I once studied with him) he taught classes at Columbus School for Girls and was given many tempting offers to

teach elsewhere, including Ohio State University. Nevertheless he chose to stay at the Art School until he retired a few years ago.

Mark and Mary added to their original lot until it totals about three acres and they created what is considered one of the loveliest informal gardens in these parts. The plot had been part of a 100-acre farm "out-lot" in the original Worthington Company survey and was owned by Moses Maynard. He had sold three quarters of an acre for $75. In 1849, apparently, this house was built and embellished with the gingerbread that has intrigued many generations. Board-and-batten vertical siding cover it. (A later owner covered the siding with stucco.) Mark designed the wing at right—a rough stone den below and half-timber, north-lighted studio above. He also added the little jewel of an entry, also in half-timber, to match the wing. The "carpenter Gothic" and old European styles blend in perfect harmony. The tiny garage and narrow driveway worked out fine, Mary says, in Model T days. Now it's a tight squeeze between paint-threatening stone walls. But there'll be no widening while the majestic maple in the sketch stands. It and the many other trees make the gingerbread house seem to be waiting for Hansel und Gretel to come out of the forest at any moment.

Mr. Hubbard's House

HIS MOTHER named him William Blackstone Hubbard, practically assuring his legal bent. Her family, the Stows of Connecticut who arrived in America in 1640, had a tendency to practice law. William was born in Utica, New York in 1795. He received "a classical collegiate education" and then read law with his uncle, Silas Stow. In 1816 he went to St. Clairsville, Ohio to practice.

His aristocratic bearing, charm and fluency served him well from the start. For several terms he served as state's attorney for Belmont County, then, at 31, was elected to the Ohio Senate. He had a passionate interest in railroads before a line was operating in the world. His 1829 bill, passed by the Ohio Legislature, is quaint in that it proposed regulating railroads in canal style: that is, "whoever owns a locomotive and cars may run them on the road upon the payment of tolls."

In 1839, Hubbard exchanged his St. Clairsville bank presidency for one in Columbus, moving to this city and becoming president of the Exchange Bank. Law was soon put aside for a perfect welter of other affairs. He became president of the first railroad into Columbus, first president of the Green Lawn Cemetery Association, president of the United States Agricultural Society, trustee of Ohio University and Grand Master of the Masonic Grand Lodge

of Ohio. He helped to draft Ohio's state banking laws.

In 1850, he built this extraordinary mansion located, according to an old directory, on the "west side of Worthington Plank Road, ½ mile north of city." His modest lot of 30 acres was on what is now called High Street. It stretched from Buttles to First and from High to Dennison. It stood tangent to a sweeping carriage circle that met High Street near First and about where Hubbard Avenue now intersects. The house was designed by imaginative Richard A. Sheldon. A year earlier Sheldon had dazzled the city with his fairyland Gothic design for Starling Medical College (later St. Francis Hospital). While completely unlike the college building, the house displayed Sheldon's love of picturesque detail.

Three years later, Capital University began its 23-year stay at High and Goodale. Later a less desirable neighbor located just south of Hubbard's land. It was the giant stable of the Columbus Street Railway Company, a horsecar outfit. By this time Hubbard was dead. He lived his strenuous life one year past the Scriptural three score and ten, dying in this house January 5, 1866.

The great house was razed, as near as I can learn, shortly after World War I. The name survives in Hubbard Avenue and Hubbard School.

Once an Auditorium

THOUSANDS of Columbus residents attended parties, plays, dances and basketball games in this building at Sixth and Oak. It was known for 40 years as the K. of C. Auditorium. It has had a remarkable second career during the last 15 years.

For nearly 150 years the plot ran from Oak to State along Sixth Street; was once owned by Alfred Kelley whose Greek Revival house stood facing Sixth Street on Broad Street. In 1850 Kelley sold the lot to Dr. Francis Carter, professor at the new Starling Medical College directly across State Street. Carter retained Richard A. Sheldon, architect for the college building, to design him a home. Sheldon turned out a delightful Gothic house that was a Columbus landmark for three quarters of a century.

In 1857 the house was bought by Ohio Governor Salmon P. Chase. Widower Chase and his bewitching but ill-fated daughter, Kate, made it a social center and hot-bed of political intrigue. Kate, at least, was determined that her father should be president. Chase did go to Washington, but as Lincoln's secretary of the treasury and, later as a Supreme Court justice. In the meantime, industrial tycoon Charles Hayden bought the house and owned it until it was sold to the Knights of Columbus in 1910.

The Knights used it as their clubhouse and in 1912 built this auditorium and connected it to the house. In 1927 they razed the old house and erected the big K. of C. Building (more recently the Catholic Youth Center).

One room of the old house remained. The northern-most chamber, it was once Governor Chase's library and scene of many political conferences. For years the sur-viving room served as a cloakroom for the auditorium. In 1952 the auditorium was sold to Byer & Bowman, Co-lumbus advertising agency. For the first time the big lot was divided and the last of the Carter-Chase-Hayden house had to bite the dust. (There is still a patch of white paint on the north wall of the Youth Center building where the old room butted against it.) Many people here and all over the country will remember that the United States billeted aviation mechanic trainees in the audi-torium building for some years during World War II.

After Byer & Bowman purchased the structure, archi-tect Mark Feinknopf transformed the cavernous interior, complete with stage, dressing rooms, fly galleries and balcony, into efficient offices. Illustrative of the changing times, part of the foundation of the ancient house sup-ports the agency's private theater for previewing televi-sion film.

Bill Arter

110 Year Old 'Central'

ONE OF the most architecturally satisfying churches in town is old Central Presbyterian on 3rd Street between State and Town. Its special picturesqueness is really the result of a catastrophe: when the building was nearing its 30th year, May 5, 1887, a roaring windstorm toppled its great spire that soared 188 feet toward heaven. A graceful curved roof replaced it and echoed most happily that of its companion tower.

For nearly a half century two of the largest Presbyterian Churches in the land stood just the width of 3rd Street apart—this one and the First Presbyterian, located where the Hartman Theater stands. In 1839 a colony left the latter, intending to form a Congregational Church. Largely in deference to famous Rev. Lyman Beecher (father of the author of "Uncle Tom's Cabin") the dissidents decided to remain Presbyterian. But they formed an Independent church, acknowledging no subjection to Presbytery, Synod or General Assembly. They had a new church built by the next year, on 3rd Street near Main. They were fortunate in a choice of their first minister, Rev. Harry L. Hitchcock who served them 15 years. A curious fact this, that three of the church's first four ministers were graduates of Yale. Hitchcock left the church to accept the presidency of Western Reserve University.

The first building was soon too small. Member Daniel

Woodbury said he would give the lot where the church now stands if it were built at once. Architect Sidney Stone was retained; he estimated a year and $35,000 were needed to build. It took two years and twice the money. Stone (the material, not the architect) was at fault. It was decided to use that material instead of brick, and to import it by canal boat. It was more costly and a long unrepaired break in the canal delayed its reaching Columbus. Eventually, April 15, 1859, the chapel was dedicated. The city fire bell was hung in the spire. It served a dual purpose as church bell and fire alarm for many years. And firemen from the old firehouse across the street used the tower to practice rescue work. When the spire fell they were delighted to find the bell unhurt in the debris. They contributed $410 toward repairing the tower and rehanging the bell. That same bell is still rung every Sunday at 9:30. A more recent addition is the electrified carillon, first played at the time of President Kennedy's death.

I roamed its interior recently, enjoying its spacious, gracious sanctuary with the sweeping balcony around three sides and the great pipe organ that really looks like a pipe organ. The lofty stained glass window in front was made and given by member Ludwig Von Gerichten. Before it was installed it went to a Chicago World's Fair, took first prize, and then toured the world, according to the pastor, Rev. John W. Omerod.

Market District Hotel

ANOTHER vanished Columbus landmark is the old Farmers Hotel. It stood on 4th Street directly across from Central Market. As its name suggests, it catered to farmers who had stands on market. It couldn't have been handier for them.

Franklin County Historical Society is publishing a booklet, *Central Market, Columbus' First City Hall*, prepared by the society's president, Walter English, and Gilbert Dodds, its research director. Among others of their findings is first-hand material on the hotel from the lips of a woman who grew up in it. Mrs. Richard Sinclair, born in Columbus in 1878, is the granddaughter of Peter Clouser, proprietor from the early 1870s until 1890.

Mrs. Sinclair remembers the market in the '80s when "most of the butchers and farmers stayed at the Farmers Hotel. They came early and got up at 4 o'clock in the morning to get their stands ready; the market opened for business at 6 a.m. . . . Tuesdays, Thursdays and Saturdays . . . on Saturday night at 9 o'clock the bell would ring and merchants could sell their remaining things at any price . . . many people waited around until late to get bargains."

I drew from a photo taken from upstairs in the markethouse at least 30 years ago. To visualize how it looked in its more glamorous days, I eliminated a clutter of stands, store front displays and outside stairways. I was startled to discover that the north wing had an extra story. Mrs. Sinclair recalls a new addition being built, probably that wing. She tells that, "The hotel had 75 rooms . . . When the state and county fairs were going, the hotel was really crowded and they put people in the halls to sleep. Rooms were only 35c for the night and meals were only 25c. For a meal, people got two kinds of meat, potatoes, a vegetable, dessert including two kinds of pie and coffee, tea or milk."

Checking old directories, I found that Peter Clouser was succeeded as proprietor by his widow in 1891. By 1900, John Clouser (presumably a son) was in the post. Subsequent proprietors, up until 1937 when the hotel is no longer listed as such, were Charles Decker, William Lloyd and Mrs. Flora Lloyd. In 1925, under Decker, it is listed as having only 75 rooms. Still later the entire ground floor was given over to businesses, including an A & P Store, with rooms to let above. Today the 12-story Holiday Inn occupies the site.

Carl Ebright told me that he covered a homicide at the Farmers Hotel about 1936, when he was a young police reporter. An outraged female guest climaxed a violent quarrel with an obstreperous visitor by throwing him downstairs. He was killed by the fall.

Ohio's Capitol Building

IT HAS BEEN called: dumpy, squat, heavy and un-lovely—all sorts of uncomplimentary things. But it was my pleasure to hear Frank Lloyd Wright describe it as "fine, the most honest of state capitols, sincere and forth-right." He would have been astounded to learn that at least seven architects had, at varying times, had a hand in its design.

The capitol building is the fourth to serve as such. Two of them were built outside Columbus, before there was a Columbus (at Chillicothe and Zanesville) and one stood at the southwest corner of the present grounds.

Not only did the building suffer architect trouble but worse: legislature trouble. The bill authorizing it was passed in 1838 and construction began the next year. In the meantime a design competition was held. Third prize winner was landscape architect Thomas Cole. His design was most nearly followed but the winner of first place, Henry Walter, was made supervising architect. He was to have four successors.

The tremendous wave of the Greek Revival was crest-ing; it was to be the style. Ohio planned to build eco-nomically by using convict labor, a fact that may have dictated a relatively simple style. A 12-foot fence was erected to safely contain the convicts. Limestone was contracted from William Sullivant's nearby quarry. (It is loaded with fossils that may still be seen in state-

house stone.) The work began with tremendous footers, up to 10 feet deep and 15 feet thick. The cornerstone, laid July 4, 1839, contains a flock of memorabilia and a scroll which begins, "The State of Ohio being the 16th state admitted to the Union . . . 1802." Both facts are in error.

Shortly thereafter a nasty situation developed. The legislature had voted to censure one of its members. He evidently was popular with Columbus' young bloods for 64 of them caused to be published a signed statement ex-pressing undiminished confidence in the censured one. Long-smoldering resentment against Columbus and its "uppity" citizens broke out in the legislature. G. B. Flood from Licking County chose the perfect moment to intro-duce his bill repealing the act for the erection of a state-house. It passed both houses handily and the work came to an abrupt halt. It was six years before a new legislature voted to resume work. It went forward under a new archi-tect, W. R. West. It was complete enough to be opened with a grand celebration January 6, 1857. By this time West had been replaced by Nathan Kelly; Kelly by Wil-liam Andrews and Andrews by Isaiah Rogers. Even with all this architectural talent, the dome (or more correctly, the lantern) has been considered incomplete by many for all the 110 years since. More about the Statehouse next week.

Statehouse and Annex

THIS view of the Statehouse, from 3rd and State Streets, features a questionable turn-of-the-century "improvement." More space was needed for state departments long before the 19th century closed. Various proposals were made, including building a new Statehouse. (The old was considered a pretty homely affair by many.) Finally it was decided to build the "Statehouse Annex" seen in the foreground of my sketch. While it provided more space, conveniently located, it ruined the imposing view of the capitol from the east. And it blocked the great East Terrace, size 73 by 210 feet, that was planned for public functions. From that proud esplanade Abraham Lincoln spoke twice: as a candidate on September 16, 1859 and as president-elect on February 13, 1861. A bronze marker may be seen at the spot.

Even before the building was completed, wrangling began over the superstructure. Alternate proposals included a "Grecian roof," a plain octagonal tower and a drum surrounded by Corinthian columns and surmounted by a dome like the National Capitol. The dome proposal has been revived at intervals ever since. Most recent serious agitation was in 1932. In 1925 it was urged that the annex be replaced with a skyscraper office building and that a new dome be installed on the Statehouse at the same time. Recently the entire interior of the rotunda has

been redesigned and refurbished so it may be assumed no further changes are planned.

The most astounding chapter in Ohio's Statehouse history has to do with an almost incredible blunder of the builders: Soon after the Civil War the proud building developed "halitosis." The stench steadily worsened and even became a health hazard as occupants contracted "Statehouse Malaria." It was blamed on a faulty ventilation system, the stabling of Civil War couriers' horses in the basement and musty records.

In 1879 an appropriation was made to correct the situation. Investigators were handicapped because there were no drawings to follow. Workmen began breaking into the flues and made a shocking discovery. Lee's *History of Ohio* relates, "In the construction of water closets in the building (a distinct novelty in the 1850s), connection had been made with the ventilating flues instead of the sewers . . . the entire system of air ducts was clogged . . . 150 barrels of filth were taken from the ducts." Needless to say, the atmosphere was greatly improved.

Most drastic change in this century is the all-but-invisible, underground parking garage which now lies beneath most of the 10-acre plot. One portal is barely discernible at left in the sketch. With fresh new grass and landscaping, the 110-year-old capitol never looked better.

St. Joseph Academy

SISTER VINCENT FETH, of the Sisters of Notre Dame de Namur, is the author of a well searched, beautifully written history of her order's first 50 years in Columbus, 1855 to 1905. I am most grateful to her and to her work for facts about St. Joseph Academy, established by the order in 1875.

Columbus' population was 18,000 in 1855. With the exception of planked High Street all thoroughfares were unpaved. The capitol building was unfinished but the city was proud of its many fine churches, among them the two quite new Catholic Churches, Holy Cross and St. Patrick's. At the request of their pastors, four of the sisters came that year and began to teach in the two church schools. Unlike some western cities, Columbus was remarkably free of religious bigotry. However, the local press had recently written darkly of "the politico-religious" organization, the Jesuits; ending a diatribe with "Even now the world sits under its shadow." Some local citizens, thus indoctrinated, whispered that perhaps these newly arrived "black-robed ladies were Jesuits in disguise." For the most part, however, they were hardly noticed as they trudged to school that first bitter cold winter from a tiny rented cottage northeast of Broad and Washington. They had two other temporary residences before 1863.

That year they built the plain but snug brick convent house at 331 East Rich Street which still stands and is in daily use. It can be seen in the center of my sketch.

Ten years later, Bishop Sylvester H. Rosecrans was urging the sisters to establish a private day school for girls. They proceeded prayerfully but with misgivings to acquire a lot just west of their house and to erect the large building seen at right in the sketch at a cost of $13,762. Their misgivings became dismay when they learned that the Dominican Sisters had accepted a similar invitation and were able to open a similar school, three blocks away, in January, 1875. (Called Sacred Heart Academy, it remained in Columbus only until 1879.) St. Joseph opened in September, 1875 with 30 pupils. Before the year was over it had enrolled 90.

By 1880 the convent house was badly overcrowded and its second-floor chapel was hopelessly inadequate. That year was built the little jewel of a chapel just back of the house, with living quarters on its top floor. In 1897 a four-story convent was built behind the chapel. The sisters' beloved garden was reduced in size but a glass-enclosed cloister helped make up for the loss. In 1925 a new high school building was added west of the academy, and in 1962 a new convent was built just east of the old house. A recent check showed it housed 63 sisters—teachers at St. Joseph, St. Agnes, St. Aloysius, St. Augustine and St. Christopher schools.

House Wheelbarrows Built

THERE was nothing square about the architecture of Felix Jacobs. Some readers will remember a previous Vignette (December 11, 1966) picturing his gigantic octagonal house at 450 East Norwich Avenue. The home sketched here with its big round tower is at 1421 Hamlet Street.

Felix was vice president of Kilbourne & Jacobs Manufacturing Company, described in an 1890 booklet as "the largest maker of earth-moving implements in the nation." This conjures up behemoth earth movers of today, but the picture is soon punctured as it goes on, "The wheelbarrow shops alone cover seven acres." They also made horse-drawn scrapers and many other devices for contractors, and they made a lot of money. The Jacobs (two brothers and a sister) could well indulge a taste for fancy housing like this gray brick mansion.

The big corner lot was really eight lots, in the Anna and Joseph Erb "Terrace Addition." Famous names had owned the land. In 1836, William Neil, the "Stagecoach King," bought 125 acres from the son of the original grantee for $4100. H. T. Chittenden bought it in 1866 and laid out "Woodburn Addition." The Erbs later bought, replatted and renamed it.

Felix bought his first lots in 1892 but was still adding and clearing title in 1901. Presumably he built this house shortly afterward. Its dominant feature is the fine, fat

tower, nearly 20 feet in diameter, and the concentric porch around it. Towers of the 1890s had been rather skinny, useless affairs but Felix's provides three big rooms —one on each floor. The house has many unusual features: A private electrical telephone system (not speaking tubes) connected several rooms. Hinged glass storm windows (some remaining in place) hung like shutters. The first floor and basement ceiling is of solid concrete. But the heating system is most notable. The original, big, double furnace and boiler, now converted to gas, still serves nobly. While the upper two floors have conventional steam radiators, the first floor is warm-air heated via curious heat exchangers in the basement. Inside the big wooden cabinet I examined were banks of steam pipes; many dozens of them. A cold air return entered the bottom and hot air registers opened from its top. The system still works perfectly. (The later octagon house experiments were less successful.) Workmanship, from brickwork to woodwork, is exquisite throughout the mansion.

In recent years the 30-room home has been divided into 11 apartments. The big coach house will soon add two more, according to owners John McIntyre and Ralph Arthur. A third building, the small circular affair seen at right in my sketch (I had to move it some yards to show it) is a complete mystery since there is no clue to its intended function.

Indianola Park

CHARLIE MILES, a dentist turned real estate man, developed Indianola Heights and Indianola Summit. Then, in 1904, he sparked a new venture at North Fourth Street and 19th. He proposed a distinct novelty—a swimming pool. Planned originally to be a modest 50 by 100 feet, it ended being a giant 140 by 238 feet, the largest pool in Ohio. It held a lot of water (1,800,000 gallons) which was supplied by four artesian wells at the rate of 30,000 gallons per hour.

While digging the builders struck quicksand. Before it was controlled a heavily loaded wagon mired. The mules were cut loose but the wagon sank out of sight and presumably is still there. The pool and a big bath house were completed and then it was decided to surmount the latter with a dance pavilion. Typical of its time, it sported towers, arcades and promenades with flags and pennants waving from every pinnacle. The place acquired a name, "Indianola Park," and began to acquire other features: a merry-go-round, a restaurant, theater, chute-the-chutes and what was claimed to be the fastest coaster of its time, the Blue Streak.

The old North Fourth Street carline (which ran in a grassy strip beside the street) ended somewhat short of the park. An injunction had been issued to prevent its extension. Mr. Miles, a man of action, gathered equipment and materials and hired a track crew. On Saturday, after the courts were closed, he went to work. The new line was completed before Monday. He escaped possible court action because the injunction had applied to the railway company and not to him as an individual.

Among the attractions at one time or another were "King and Queen, the High Diving Horses," Cromwell Dixon and his airship (which got away from the park and sailed far south of the city), Keith Vaudeville acts, an operating model of the Panama Canal and a flea circus operated by a Yale graduate. Carl Randall, who became a great Ziegfeld star, began his dancing at Indianola. J. Real Neth was roller coaster man, Phil Bucklew was pool manager and Jack Fullen was a lifeguard. Late in the park's career, Kit Carson, Ken Jones and Phil Dusenbury leased the pavilion and ran it as "Club Playmore" with Kit as featured vocalist and a full bill of acts.

When the pool was opened, I was told, "Hardly a hundred Columbus women could swim." Maidenly modesty, too, kept them away. For a time Miles offered $2 to women who would enter the pool and stay 20 minutes. He also erected a long canopy from bath house to pool so they could enter the water waist deep before being seen. Even so, the ladies who dared came attired in knee-length suits.

The pool and pavilion continued in operation until 1937, then closed. Later the remains became a shopping center with the pavilion a supermarket which still can be seen today.

The Jeffrey Mansion

THE JEFFREY MANSION at 165 North Parkview in Bexley is much like fabled English country houses (Hardwick Hall, where Mary Queen of Scots was imprisoned, and famous Haddon Hall, for instance). Those seats of great British families were appropriate models for this, the estate of a distinguished American family.

Joseph A. Jeffrey founded Jeffrey Manufacturing Company in 1883. Thanks to his efforts, its growth was fantastic. His son, Robert H., displayed the same furious energy. It is well displayed in the story of his education: Born in Columbus in 1873, Robert went to Douglas School, studied two years in Dresden, Germany, and then at Columbus Latin School. At 17, he entered Williams College where he graduated. Then for a year he worked in the coal mines of Ohio and Illinois and returned to work in Jeffrey's drafting room and its chain shop. While so employed he walked to work at crack of dawn, left the plant early enough to walk to OSU and study law, then walked downtown to attend night classes at Columbus Business College. It would seem that he earned his rapid rise in the company.

In 1903, at 29, he became a candidate for mayor. His opponent, John Hinkle, laughed at the rich boy's pretensions and pinned on him the tag, "Little Lord Fauntleroy." In spite of the derision, he was elected by a large majority. He served his term, "a businesslike and pro-gressive administration," then declined to be renominated. The factory was taking more and more of his time.

While he was mayor, Robert began this house, designed by Frank Packard. Its setting, in the British tradition, is a spacious, wooded "park" of many acres, running from Parkview to Alum Creek. The mansion is spectacularly located at the end of a long, wide drive, flanked by big trees and ending at the principal entrance in a circle. Its style, Tudor, was developed in England after the feudal period when there was no longer need for high blank walls and provisions for defense. It is characterized by great banks of windows, strong emphasis on horizontals and the combining of stone and brick. Authorities say there is no finer example in the country.

Robert twice added to his home. In 1922 he built the many-windowed entrance wing which contains a monumental stone stairway. It was completed in time for him to watch the approach of visiting President Harding from a landing.

In 1926 north and south wings and the stately terrace at the back were added. In 1941, he gave the house and vast estate to the city of Bexley to be used as a unique and magnificent community center. Robert H. Jeffrey II told me that the avenue of pin oaks, now huge trees, was planted by his grandfather in the 1920s. They have grown mightily.

Thurber's Ghost House

THIS sturdy brick structure at 77 Jefferson Avenue looks like anything but a house once haunted by a ghost. Yet I have in front of me a signed statement by a former resident that it was.

Jefferson Avenue was named for our third president, perhaps because his signature appears on the first deed to the land. It was one of the most elegant streets of the first super-elegant addition to the city—East Park Place, platted in 1870. This house probably was built in 1873 when its owner got a $1600 loan from the Home Building and Loan Association. After a couple of transactions, it was bought by an absentee owner and had different tenants for many years.

From 1913 until 1917 it was the home of Mr. and Mrs. Charles Thurber and their three sons. One of the sons, the late James Thurber, then an OSU student, became one of America's greatest humor writers. It was he who told of the spirit visit in "The Night the Ghost Got In," probably the most hilarious ghost story ever written. I accepted the story as pure invention.

Some years ago I was writing a piece about Thurber's years in Columbus and noted some discrepancies among addresses he has mentioned. For instance, he placed the ghost house at 77 Lexington Avenue while my research showed it to be at 77 Jefferson Avenue. I wrote him my questions and got a delightful answer—with this startling explanation: "I deliberately changed the address for the simple reason that there *was* a ghost . . . The family who lived in the house ahead of us moved out because of the strange sounds, we found out later. A corner druggist near the house, to whom I related my experience, described the walking and the running upstairs before I could describe it myself. They were undeniably the steps of a man, and it was quite an experience to hear him running up the stairs toward us, my brother and me, and to see nothing whatever. A Columbus jeweler is said to have shot himself in the house after running up those steps. This is the only authentic ghost I ever encountered myself and we never heard it again . . . I didn't want to alarm whoever might be living there when I wrote the story. I think it was a music school for girls." (The house *was* listed in the 20s as "The Wallace Collegiate School and Conservatory of Music.")

That was an obviously very serious Thurber writing. But his story must have exorcised the ghost for I can find no one who has heard it since. Mrs. Marie Madry, who has owned the house for 19 years and who used to live there, says quite firmly, "No ghosts."

If you want to read Thurber's story, you'll find it in the book, *The Thurber Carnival*.

Castle on the Campus

BY 1896 OHIO State University had grown "huge," had nearly a thousand students, needed an armory, gymnasium and a place big enough to hold graduation. It was decided to satisfy all these needs with one quite grand building. The trustees selected as architects the firm of Yost and Packard.

It is impossible to say who chose medieval-castle style (hardly Frank Packard) but such was the decision, and the firm did it up brown. Essentially the building was a great, iron-arched shed nearly hidden behind walls, towers and turrets topped with crenelations to protect the archers should it be necessary to defend it. To a generation infatuated with towers and romantic embellishments, it must have seemed a dream about to come true.

Columbus Construction Company got the job on a bid so low that the trustees were worried. The worry was justified for early in 1897 the firm gave up. The trustees then completed the structure. The merest glance at its intricate brickwork must have (and probably did) scare off most contractors. From indications, it cost nearly twice what had been bid.

At ground level was the big, 80-by-150-foot, "drill hall." Above that was a canvas running track with 750 seats surrounding it. In the basement were athletic facilities including two pools (men's and women's). The men's was 17½ by 30 feet. The women's was even smaller and was called a "plunge bath." James A. Pollard, university historian who helped me with facts, remembers a time when all men had to swim twice the length of the pool to graduate. It must not have had a filtration system; it was drained and filled daily; scrubbed thrice each week. Also in the basement were: "lecture room, bicycle room and cannon room."

Famous ROTC commandant Col. George L. Converse had his office in the base of the largest tower. "Connie" is remembered for his autocratic rule and his one glittering eye. The other, covered with an eye patch, still had a bullet in it acquired during Indian warfare.

For a long time the trustees refused use of the Armory for boy-girl affairs. But for some years it was the scene of an annual Coed Prom—an all-coed dance with half the girls dressed as boys. (This was before things got so confused in that department.) A terrible fuss was precipitated when one coed sneaked her boy friend in "disguised as a boy."

The Armory came to be despised by many in later generations for its frowning pretensions, though some of us didn't agree.

It suffered at least two fires, the first in 1935. The second and fatal fire struck in the early morning hours, May 16, 1958. It was said to be damaged beyond repair. Arson was suspected but never proved. And it is hard to believe anyone hated it that much. It was razed during the ensuing summer.

'The Octagon Mode'

MOST Columbus residents have passed within yards of this house at 2130 East Broad many times without seeing it. Located on a knoll, well back, and screened by shrubs and trees, it is immediately east of Sessions Village.

The land on which it stands was once part of the far-flung Nelson family holdings. Later it was owned by Samuel Barr and then Elizabeth Barr. She inherited it in 1853, and that year, it is believed, the house was built. In 1880 it was bought by Columbus banker and entrepreneur, Francis Sessions. It was known as the Sessions farmhouse until his death in 1892. It remained in possession of his widow, Orange Johnson's daughter, Mary, until her death in 1919. The eight walls are of brick and stone, now stuccoed. Interior woodwork is all of black walnut and cherry. Its kitchen was evidently in the basement originally; the connecting dumb waiter still exists.

Almost certainly its octagon plan was the result of a book, freshly published at the time of its building, titled in part, "The Octagon Mode of Building." Other octagon houses that dot Ohio and many parts of the country are known to have been so inspired. Even at this late date, reading its yellowed pages (a copy was loaned to me by John and Lucille Spurrier) one is half convinced of the superiority of the octagon over the square. The author proves, for instance, that, with no increase in total wall length, one-fifth more space is enclosed. And that is only a beginning. He claims the octagon house is stronger, lighter, easier to heat and ventilate and far more handsome. On the latter point his argument is of doubtful merit today: "Some forms," he says, "are constitutionally more beautiful than others. Of these the spherical is more beautiful than the angular . . . why is it that a poor animal or a lean person is more homely than the same animal or person when fleshy? Because the latter are less angular and more spherical than the former."

Still others of the author's claims become suspect as one continues. He makes a great case for glass as the ideal roofing material, offering his plan for installing such a roof cheaply. Even though he never tried it he suggests, "Cast it on the roof by having small, portable (glass) furnaces . . . and melt and run your sand, saltpeter and potash on the spot, and all in one solid sheet." At this point I checked the architectural credentials of the author, O. S. Fowler and found he had none; he was, in fact, a phrenologist.

In the 1920's Francis Fulton added an east and a west wing to this particular octagon. Now owned by the Ralston Werums, it is one of the most pleasant homes I've visited in many a day—even if it doesn't have a solid glass roof.

'Timbrook'

PEOPLE who urged me to do a "Vignette" on this house described it as a "Southern colonial mansion on Olentangy River Road." Not too long ago they would have been wrong on both counts. It acquired its two-story portico and classical details about 1923, when it was already nearing 50 years of age. And its address until the 1930's was "Meek Road." (Present address is 5811 Olentangy River Road.)

From early times a road existed along the west bank of the river. The road divides just north of Bethel Road with the left fork leading to Linworth. Until the late 30's *this* was Olentangy River Road and the present Olentangy Road, from the fork to Route 161, was called Meek Road. It was "unimproved" and almost impassable in bad weather.

This house was built about 1875 by Nelson Hoyt. It was big and roomy. With its 83 acres (including the site of present Indian Hills) it was sold for the not-so-small sum of $12,000 in 1886. Dun and Jennie Williams bought it in 1890. Anna Williams Ruppersberg told me she was born there, remembers fondly its 14 spacious rooms, the big shady lawn and orchard north of the house — and the isolation in bad weather.

In 1921 the widowed Jennie Williams sold the place to the late Everett Antrim. Antrim, one of the founders of the famous Furnas Ice Cream Company, came to Columbus from Indianapolis in 1905. He became president of Furnas with 11 plants from St. Louis to Akron. When the company was sold to Borden he become that firm's Midwest Division manager. He devoted some three years to remodeling the house, adding the big south wing, the portico and making interior changes. His son, Jack Antrim, remembers adventurous trips to check on progress. Now and then his mother drove her electric car (with some misgivings about the batteries lasting for the trip). Jack said the road was paved and electric service supplied about 1924 when they moved in. He remembers his dad's partiality for the Stearns-Knight car. Its sleeve-valve engine and the oil of the day made winter starting a real problem. His dad solved it by installing a "pot belly" stove in the garage and keeping a roaring fire going on cold nights.

In 1925 Antrim sold the house and 15 acres to George W. Timmons. The Timmons family, enthusiastic horsemen all, christened their place "Timbrook" and made its sign a jumping horse. They modified the house, too — notably adding a sunlit, "primitive"" family room at the southwest corner. Its open timbers came from the Stoddard farm near Charleston Avenue and North High Street. Doors and woodwork throughout the house are of black walnut harvested on the farm. Jack Antrim recalls that once there were even great stretches of rail fence of that same now-precious wood.

Gideon Hart House

GIDEON HART'S widowed mother, resident of Farmington, Connecticut, was granted land in far-off Ohio for the Revolutionary War services of her husband. The grant of 150 acres was made in 1800. Gideon grew up to fight in America's second war with the British—1812-1814. Soon afterwards he came to Ohio and located the grant in what was then Harrison Township but since 1824 has been Blendon Township.

In 1819 he erected Franklin County's first sawmill and the next year, several old records agree, built this house of his own sawed lumber. (These records prove something of an embarrassment for me. In a previous Vignette, September 18, 1966, I pictured the 1823 Phelps House on Granville Road and called it "Blendon's Oldest." If the Hart house *was* built in 1820, I was obviously wrong.) Whatever the truth, this house is one of the finest of its kind hereabouts. It is located at 7328 Hemstead Road.

Gideon prospered both at farming and his profession as a surveyor. He is said to have laid out Westerville, which lies just northwest. Gradually he acquired more land until his farm totaled 380 acres. Very early he planted a fine apple orchard near the house. At the southern edge of his land, in a great grove of sugar maples, he built a celebrated sugar house that even appears on early maps. Gideon was much looked up to;

was made justice of the peace and a colonel of militia. (Many military meetings were held in this house.) A man of cultured tastes, his library of 142 volumes was the wonder of the neighborhood. He died in 1859. His only son, Henry Clay Hart, and a daughter, Candace, took over the farm. Neither married and the name died with them.

The farm was subsequently owned in turn by William Phelps, a Dr. Bowman, and Emmett Fickell who bought it 1928. Mr. and Mrs. Fickell did a magnificent job of restoring the long-neglected house: removing a dozen layers of paint from its walnut and butternut woodwork, refinishing the wide ash floors, sending to Holland for missing Delft tiles for the huge kitchen fireplace and re-installing its original cooking crane. They also installed the first baths and central heating, as well as adding a wing at the back.

In 1959 the Robert L. Bayntons bought the house and added touches of their own by enclosing the room at right and installing paneled wainscoting, shutters and new exterior clapboards. The result of all this loving attention is breathtaking beauty for a house nearly 150 years old. I'm sometimes accused of "prettying up" some of my subjects (which is true) but Gideon Hart's house took none of that. It couldn't have looked better in its palmiest days.

Maggie Fager Library

FRANK AND MAGGIE FAGER started their little grocery before the turn of the century in a frame building at 969 West Broad Street. They worked hard and prospered. As the store grew it became a neighborhood gathering place presided over by the warm-hearted couple. Then, in 1912, Maggie died.

Frank mourned his helpmate and was determined to create a memorial to her. It was to be something to bring pleasure to their good West Side friends. At last he hit upon the idea of a free neighborhood library — *The Maggie Fager Memorial Library*. His lawyer and administrator of his will, John M. Lewis, arranged the details before Frank died in 1916.

In 1918 the library opened in the building that had so long housed the Fager grocery. The trustees erected a false front of brick with the library's name (I've exaggerated it a bit) chiseled in stone. There were just 50 books to start with. Sarah E. Lewis (John's sister) agreed to serve as librarian "on a strictly temporary basis." Last December she died at nearly 100, after serving as librarian for just short of half a century.

I've long been intrigued by the library's name (like something out of Dickens) and wondered about its story. When I visited it recently, gracious Mrs. Meryl Krinn showed me about. Presently it boasts more than 13,000 volumes, mostly fiction. Banks of shelves and tops of tables are filled with books, many testifying by their well worn covers to hundreds of readings by library patrons.

Mrs. Krinn, long Miss Lewis' assistant, is now librarian. She laughed at my question about a card catalog, explaining, "Don't need one. I've read every book in here, know what they are and where each one is." A woman stopped in as we talked, left a book and said she'd be back. Mrs. Krinn said they'd have a little "book talk" when she returned. "She likes books of poetry," Mrs. Krinn remarked. (It's an intimate sort of library and the librarian knows the tastes of hundreds of patrons.) It may be the only library around that does a lively business in *Tarzan, Tom Swift* and *Frank Merriwell.* "Lots of people still call for them," said Mrs. Krinn.

An interesting postscript is this: The Fager estate administrator, Lewis, seems to have fancied the library-memorial idea himself. When he died in 1954, after 55 years of practicing law, he left a considerable estate. More than $100,000 was left to establish the "Lewis Memorial Library" on West Broad Street between Sandusky and Central. The bequest was to become effective after his sister, Sarah died. It is to be built and administered by the Columbus Library.

While this would seem to over-library the area, chairman of the Fager Library board, Creth D. Irwin, says the new library will not affect their operation; that they will go on serving the near West Side as they have for nearly 50 years.

The Snow House

PEOPLE passing this house with a casual glance nearly always pause for a double take. For, although there's not the sign of a crack in its solid brick walls, the window and door frames have assumed the oddest angles, appearing to deny the inflexibility of brick and mortar. But just as we aging folk are forgiven a tendency to sag here and there, so we must surely excuse it in a house now aged precisely a century and a half. Located at 41 West New England in Worthington, it has always been known (for its builder) as "The Snow House."

John Snow was born in Providence, Rhode Island, in the Revolutionary War year of 1780. At 14 he was apprenticed to a jewelry maker. Seven years of apprenticeship and several years as a journeyman nearly ruined his eyes. He became a merchant and apparently prospered. In 1809 he took the step that colored all his life and led to what fame may be claimed for him these many years later: He became a Mason; not merely a good Mason but a perfectly passionate one, to be known by his contemporaries as "the greatest ritualist of his day."

Snow came to Worthington in 1817 and immediately built this house. It is like hundreds of others except for its most noteworthy interior feature: In the room to the right of the entry are two deep alcoves flanking the fireplace. Each is framed by delicate pilasters supporting arches. In each arch, exaggerated, is the keystone of masonry. It is said that lodge meetings were held in this room

for some time before the now-ancient Masonic Temple was built (1820-1827). Snow's vast knowledge of masonry made him master of Worthington's 15-year-old New England Lodge No. 4 his second year in town. He continued in the office four years and had to battle to be allowed to step down. In the meantime he was elected grand master of the Grand Lodge of Ohio and held that position five years. He was the prime mover in building the Worthington temple and resumed its mastership from 1827 to 1832.

Royal Arch Masonry in Ohio began in this house and Snow organized in it the first commandery of Knights Templar in the Northwest Territory—The Mount Vernon Commandery No. 1. He supported his family by operating a drugstore but his heart and most of his energy were devoted to his lodge. He died, full of honors, in his 72nd year.

Dr. J. H. Blackburn, whose offices now occupy the venerable house, showed me some of its features, including the center-hall stair of black walnut with curly maple treads, the random ash floors (that are dowelled together and laid over walnut subflooring) and a wide door of a single walnut board. I crept by flashlight down to the tiny cellar and inspected the whole, unpeeled log joists and the remains of a spring that once kept food cool. The wing seen at the left is comparatively modern. It was built during the Civil War.

Confederate Memorial

NOW AND then a stranger, passing along Sullivant Avenue between Binns and Powell, catches a glimpse of this lone sculptured figure above a stone wall and stops to investigate. To his surprise he finds it the center of a considerable cemetery—for Confederate soldiers! How it came to be is a poignant story.

In June, 1861, a large military camp was created "on the National Road, four miles west of the Capitol." Its 160 acres lay between West Broad and Sullivant. It was plowed, harrowed, rolled and finally packed hard by the tramp of thousands of feet as recruits poured in. It was named Camp Chase in honor of former Ohio Governor Salmon P. Chase.

On the site, soon afterward, a high stockade was built (300 by 700 feet) and Camp Chase began its career as a war prison. It was to become nearly as infamous to Southerners as Andersonville was to the North. Conditions at first were tolerable. But, as more and more captured Confederates were jammed in (8000 in 1863), life became increasingly wretched. During three years 5000 of them died there. Most were buried in this plot.

When the war ended Camp Chase was quickly abandoned, buildings were dismantled and sold and the land once more was farmed. Only the grim cemetery with its rail fence and plank headstones remained. More than half the bodies were removed by relatives, but 2260 remained. In 1879 the plot was deeded to the government by the executors of John G. Holloway. Then began a long period of neglect. Ohio Governor Foraker built a rude stone wall around it and installed the big boulder. But the cemetery was largely forgotten. Enter then one William H. Knauss.

Knauss, a wounded Union veteran, came to Columbus in 1893 and was shocked to find this burial place of his late foes a tangle of brush and brambles. He was particularly outraged to think that these soldiers of the great rebellion were utterly ignored on Decoration Day. And he did something about it.

Knauss worked and hired help to clean up the plot. He tried to organize a memorial service but only a handful came. Even ex-Confederates shunned it for fear of Northern prejudice. The third service, in 1898, was, however, hugely attended. The Spanish-American War was wiping out regional differences. Flowers came in by the ton, many from the South. School children sang and the GAR drummed, bugled and fired a salute. Tennessee's ex-governor spoke as did a Northern and Southern soldier.

1902 was the biggest year of all. Governor Nash spoke as well as a former GAR commander. Indefatigable William Knauss was master of ceremonies and his daughter helped a "Daughter of the Confederacy" unveil the handsome monument that is lettered simply "AMERICANS."

Medicine Man's House

THIS HOME stood at Town and Washington Streets until 1963. It was the Hartman House, built at the turn of the century by Dr. Samuel Brubaker Hartman, purveyor of the most successful nostrum in history.

Columbus is loaded with Hartman lore (and Hartman structures), some true, some half true and some entirely false. In 1961, after painstaking research, Jean Kahler wrote the definitive story of Hartman; the meagerness of his childhood, opulence of his old age and the magic word that wrought the change—"Pe-Ru-Na!" I have mined that history (published during 1961 by *The Dispatch Sunday Magazine* in seven installments) for nuggets in this and subsequent Vignettes on Hartman subjects. I'm most grateful for her research.

This house came late in the Hartman story, when the medicine, Peruna, was grossing $100,000 a day—largely profit for the doctor. He started with a modest structure, built in 1883 by Henry C. Lonnis, a hardware merchant. Hartman had bought it to live in 10 years later. By 1899, with a river of gold flowing in, he decided to splurge. For all his fine education, he is said to have feared an old German superstition that death would visit the man who built a mansion late in life. Hartman, on the eve of his 70th birthday, played it cool. He remodeled. But what a job of remodeling!

Some say he literally encased the older house in its grand new shell of light tan brick and marble, then tore out the interior and rebuilt it. The costliest materials went in; not only on the first floor but on every floor including the third where he fashioned a ballroom and theater for his stage-struck only child, Maribel. Fine as it was inside, the "outworks" were even more impressive: Gleaming white marble trim, ballustrades, pillars and a fabulous fence—a white marble wall pierced with great portholes for all its length.

Just before it was razed (but still locked up) I eased through the coal cellar window and explored. Woodwork was heavy and ornate. The richest carving was cherrywood sculpture in the huge dining room. It seemed to have an endless series of rooms. There were, as I remember, seven bedrooms (some were suites) on the second floor. But "bathroom mania" had not yet struck America for there was but a single bathroom. The house itself was kept clean by Madame Hartman's edict: No one could tread its elegant floors and carpets in shoes. Guests were given slippers to wear.

Thomas Giller told Jean Kahler that he came to make a 20-minute electrical repair and that he was kept waiting for two hours while Mrs. Hartman ordered and had sent from Lazarus a pair of slippers. She told him they'd be there for him to don whenever he came. He never went back.

Hartman's Dream Farm

NOT many of us live to see our dearest dream come true. Samuel Hartman did. Consider his unlikely beginnings: Fatherless shortly after birth (1830); farmed out at 5 to be a woodchopper; an apprentice carpenter, speaking only German, at 14 and a college hopeful at 21 with only six months of formal schooling.

He did get to college—three of them, with many interruptions—and was graduated from Jefferson Medical School in Philadelphia. After 10 years' practice he had piled up a six-figure fortune—and lost it. Then for 20 years he was a traveling "advertising physician." In the meantime he founded a little firm to make a medicine called "Pe-Ru-Na." It made most anyone who took it feel good. The fact that it was 56 to 60 proof alcohol may have helped. People who wouldn't touch whisky downed Peruna with an easy conscience and helped the product to become "the largest selling medicine in the world."

In 1890, Hartman gave up traveling and settled in Columbus where Peruna was made. For a time he kept his hand in by operating his celebrated "Surgical Hotel" but soon gave himself over to the joys of being rich. He built a mansion and big downtown buildings. But his grandest dream-come-true was his Hartman Farm, straddling for miles the Chillicothe Road (Route 23), just south of Columbus. He started with 2400 acres in 1903. In a

few years it was 5000 acres and "the largest intensely cultivated, diversified farm in the world."

Under his watchful eye the farm sprouted a seemingly endless procession of buildings: Houses, hotels, barns of every description, poultry houses, a great dairy building, a power plant, a water plant, grain elevators, machine and blacksmith shops and a red brick schoolhouse. Enclosing his "empire" were 40 miles of white board fence. He employed 250 hands, including a poor, feeble soul who was hired to pick up feathers in the duck pens. He bred three strains of horses: Arabian, German Coach and French Percheron; had the world's largest herd of registered Jersey cattle; built an electric railway to Columbus and supplied the city's milk. Thousands of visitors came. One old-timer said, "It was like the state fair every day." They rode his railway, lived in his hotels and went home filled with wonders.

The center of the farm (and scene of my sketch), once called "Spangler's Hill," is the highest point for miles around. As the "Hartman Crest," it soon took on the look of a city. Hartman is supposed to have planted the catalpa tree (the largest I ever saw) in the foreground.

Sam Keller, of Ohio National Bank's trust department, told me there are still 2200 acres upon which some 20 employes raise corn, soybeans, grapes and fruits as well as beef cattle.

Perunaville

DR. SAMUEL HARTMAN'S wonderful elixir, Peruna, was described by the doctor as "herbal drugs dissolved in a liquid made by the fermentation of juices of vegetable origin." This wonderful solvent is more commonly called alcohol. Peruna's solvent content ran from 28 to 30 per cent (56 to 60 proof alcohol). The higher proof was maintained in winter, whether as anti-freeze during shipping or because the customers preferred it a bit richer in cold weather.

It was no secret that many Peruna fanciers consumed the medicine more for its immediate effect than for its touted curative powers. The directions suggested moderation: "A tablespoonful every 3 to 6 hours." (Teething infants were allowed 30 to 60 drops in water four times daily.) Sturdier quaffers had an out: "For hysteria, a wineglass full in hot water, to be repeated as necessary." Thus all the thirsty needed was a case of hysterics and the sky was the limit.

The source of this wonderful stuff was right here at Third and Rich Streets (both sides of Third Street for half a block). Both the buildings I've sketched here are standing and were part of "Perunaville." The slightly medieval structure on the right was mostly stables for the wonderful teams used to haul Peruna by the wagon to the railroad. Across Third Street is the classic-detailed, white administration building with "PERUNA" still chiseled above the first floor. It was started in 1902 (I've heard that famous Sanford White designed it).

It was incomplete but in use for storage, packing and shipping in 1904 when sparks from a workman's torch ignited some excelsior. The conflagration that followed threatened the whole end of town. Thousands of bottles of Peruna went up with a whoosh. Loss was estimated at $50,000. "Ruined and no insurance," said the newspapers. But it was only a temporary setback. Hartman rebuilt at once, and by 1906, when the building was in full use, Peruna was outselling every medicine in the United States.

Employes didn't share too handsomely in the profits (though they had the privilege of buying dollar bottles of Peruna for 60 cents). Jane McGill, who worked in the advertising department, said, "We worked from 7 until 5 on weekdays and from 7 until 4 on Saturdays for $10 a week." On Christmas Day, employes were docked a day's pay, then given a silver dollar as a gift.

Hartman, his son-in-law, Frederick Schumacher, and Peruna were riding high in 1906, but that was the year disaster struck—disaster in the form of an order (by the United States government) to either reduce the alcoholic content or market the product as an alcoholic beverage.

The Compleat Man

JAMES E. WRIGHT, who built this house at 259 East Granville Road in Worthington, was a member of that noble race which mastered most of the learning of his time. The son of a Dublin farmer who read and loved the classics, he devoured books from earliest childhood. His first job paid three dollars a month—promptly spent for books. At 12, it is told, he had already mastered 13 arithmetic and mathematics books, subjects he loved all his life. Before he died at 61, he had been a teacher, engineer, author, attorney, artisan, treasurer and man who cherished knowledge for itself.

Wright was born in 1829 near Dublin, Ohio. Largely by his own efforts he attended Central College, Wittenberg and Ohio Wesleyan. As the merest youth he taught himself surveying and was made a civil engineer during construction of the Cleveland, Lorain & Wheeling Railroad. At 16 he entered Princeton where he distinguished himself by writing stories and essays published by leading magazines. Their quality was high enough to draw praise from the great Washington Irving. At 19 his eyesight failed and he had to leave college. Later Princeton granted him a master's degree.

Wright studied law under Sam Galloway in Columbus. His sight was improving but he had to have the law cases read to him. Yet he passed the bar examination handily in 1853. Two years later, as his law practice flourished, he married Elizabeth Davis of Dublin. In 1869 he moved to Worthington and built the first portions of this house. That same year he was appointed to fill an unexpired term as treasurer of Franklin County, an office to which he was later twice elected.

A student all of his life, he "spoke Latin better than a priest," studied and enjoyed calculus and engineering and read "practically every book in print." He had a gigantic library and "the best-equipped workshop" a visitor had ever seen. (A corner of it is visible at right in my sketch.)

The Wrights had eight children, nearly all of whom distinguished themselves. They became college professors, a school superintendent, a minister, writers, lawyers and presidents of a corporation. Their colleges included Yale, Cornell, Columbia, Ohio State, Armour and Oberlin. Moses Wright, youngest child and last one to survive, died in Washington, D.C. in 1965. He had succeeded his older brother, Paul, as president of the Realty Title Insurance Company of that city.

The grand old house has had many additions and acquired its steamboat Gothic embellishments in the 1880s. Mrs. Harriet Martin, a cousin of Moses Wright, showed me through its dozen or more rooms—most with marble fireplaces of differing designs—full of Victorian furniture, books and bric-a-brac. It stands on 10 acres, largely wooded, to provide the quiet and solitude in the heart of town that James Wright craved in his later years.

Westcrest on the Gahanna

WESTCREST is the name they gave it because it was built on the west side of the Gahanna River (Big Walnut) at the crest of the long rise from that stream. It was built by David Taylor between 1840 and 1843. David's father, Robert, had brought his family to this area (then silent forest) in 1809. It came to be called "Truro Woods" because the Taylors emigrated from Truro, Nova Scotia. Later the township was named Truro. Westcrest is at 5300 East Main Street.

Unlike most ancient houses, Westcrest has undergone no basic changes. It was conceived, happily, as you see it today. Perfectly symmetrical, built sturdily of brick made on the site, it has stood thus for a century and a quarter. The David Taylors remained only until 1858, then moved to the house still occupied by the family at 1400 East Broad.

Westcrest had various tenants for a decade, and then for 20 years became the home of the Strahl family. In 1888 Henry Phalor moved his family in to begin a 36-year stay. He cultivated the big 360-acre Taylor farm but also found time to beautify the grounds of his home.

I had the unusual experience of joining a dozen Phalor descendants at Westcrest in what became a kind of impromptu reunion. Five of them had lived there (there were 11 children) and exclaimed over each rediscovery—the foundation of the old water tower their father had installed, the pair of giant maples that were huge even in the 90's, the little milkhouse and the big, dressed stone that had once supported a sundial. The quaint little brick smokehouse is gone without a trace. They were distressed at the overgrown look and showed me pictures of the elegant lawn taken when they lived there. One of the five, Chester, pointed out the beautiful front stairway where he "met a ghost long ago." Much family discussion down the years has never shaken his story. No one has ever had any except a ghostly explanation for the stranger he met there.

The Phalors explained the arrangement of the house. The left wing was the sitting room and across the front of the center was the formal parlor. The right wing was the back parlor. There were two bedrooms on the first floor and four on the second. The kitchen and dining room were in back and below the main level. The lot fell steeply from the front so they were at ground level.

From the 1920's until last year, the Columbus Riding Club leased 100 acres adjoining Westcrest where it built a clubhouse and indoor arena. (A fragment is visible at right.) For many years the house was operated as a restaurant called "The Farmhouse," later taken over by the Riding Club. It still belongs to the Taylor family.

'Premo De Orient'

SIXTY-odd years ago establishments like this were tacitly recognized if not universally approved. Columbus had a number of areas that were lumped as "red light districts." But this one, around Grant and Mound, was really above that designation.

Along these quiet streets were the aristocrats among houses of amatory dalliance. Half a dozen famous madames presided over their decorous, sophisticated resorts within a block. (There were Clara Stage, Edith Stanton, Maud Wilson and Nora Bell, each with her name displayed on her door.) But not one of these could compare in swank and luxury with this tall house at 338 South Grant. The costly etched glass of its twin doors bore the most famous name of all: "Vinnie Grey."

Vinnie, a beautiful, imperious girl from a sleepy, southern Ohio village, came to the city and made good in a spectacular way. By the early 1900's she was mistress of "Premo De Orient," as she styled the house I've sketched. (I sat in a field of thigh-high grass on slum clearance land to draw the sadly run-down street.)

Behind its severe facade was unbelievable luxury and fantasy. Astonishingly, Vinnie actually published a brochure picturing its wonders in detail. With amazement I leafed through it and saw why the richest young bloods of Columbus considered entry to Vinnie's a privilege without equal. On each page is a single large photo with simple identification. "Front Hall" shows the classic, tile-lined foyer with a statue lamp and bas-reliefs. (I have heard that a formally-attired butler presided over the entrance.)

The sumptuous "Private Parlor" had great mural panels featuring nudes, rich furniture and bric-a-brac. The "Turkish Room" was all aswirl in heavy hangings with a deeply cushioned and tented alcove, shields, crossed weapons, scent lamps and thick Oriental rugs.

"Big Square" was a spacious party room with gigantic mirrors to multiply the fun and Louis XIV furniture. Most pretentious was the vast, glittering "Ballroom." Mirror-lined, it had velvet benches around all the walls. Long-ago visitors told me the girls were all in evening dress and that talented ones peformed on the grand piano.

Other entertainment rooms ranged from awesomely thematic to simply cozy. Seven pages are of richly furnished bedrooms on the third floor. Baths, proudly included, featured high, clawfoot tubs and mammoth lavatories. It's no wonder old-timers have told me, "New York had nothing finer."

I've known about Vinnie's for a long time. Now, with some misgivings, I present it—as authentic Americana, part of a way of life now gone. My decision is hastened by the fact that it is doomed, very soon, to be destroyed by fire as a part of a fire department experiment. Thus it will provide one last extravaganza before ceasing to be.

Professor Guitner's House

SUBURBAN Westerville has many excellent potential Vignette subjects. This one is known to older local folk as "The Guitner House," for the family who owned it for 77 years.

The original house (at 75 West College Avenue) was a one-floor, two-room affair built by Lewis and Rebecca Davis in 1849. In 1856 and again in 1869 they remodeled, adding a second story and other first-floor rooms. In 1874 the house was bought by John E. Guitner, 33-year-old professor of Greek and Latin at Otterbein College.

His wife, Lydia Winter Guitner, a talented musician, had the first piano in town and played the first organ in the college chapel. Husband, wife and daughter were all professors at the college. Mrs. Guitner taught instrumental music and their daughter, Alma, taught German language and literature after completing her schooling in Berlin. For 71 continuous years one or more Guitners taught at Otterbein.

The house attracts unusual people. It was coveted and bought, in 1951, by Robert and Clara Creager, both artists. Bob owns a successful commercial art studio. Clara is principally interested in weaving, and exhibits regularly. They took me on a tour of the house, which

by now has become a very "rambly" sort of residence.

The most recent addition is the long, low wing at right which the Creagers built for their at-home studio. Out back is a delightful paved courtyard centering on a giant dug well (still producing cold, pure water) and shaded by a famous grape arbor. When the college burned, long ago, Professor Guitner held class in the east front room, adjoining on fine days to the courtyard. One of the cherished memories of those students are of the idyllic hours in the cool shade with their much-loved professor.

Picturesque from any angle, the house is seen at its best from the front where its carpenter Gothic details can be admired. They are unique and the most intricate I have ever seen.

The house is crisply and elegantly kept but my perverse nature prompted me to "weather" it a bit, as it might have been now and then when an absent-minded professor forgot to have it painted. More likely there were years when he couldn't afford it for his salary was never greater than $1200 a year. A gentle, dedicated scholar, money wasn't important to him. He lived most contentedly all his life teaching at his own alma mater and dying just as the new century began.

Washington's Messenger

WE IN OHIO are likely to feel we have few ties to the Revolutionary War. Yet much of our state was given by a more or less grateful government to veterans of that conflict. From my perusal of old titles it seems that few of them occupied the lands so given. Often they sold or traded them to others, most often to land speculators. Yet many did come and their bones rest in Ohio soil.

Among the most notable of such were John and Ann Davis, both veterans of the war that freed America. Ann's name is proudly perpetuated by Franklin County's Ann Simpson Davis Chapter of the DAR. I was fortunate enough to learn the history of the remarkable girl and woman from her great-great-granddaughter, Mrs. Harriet C. Martin, an organizing member of the chapter.

Ann Simpson was a beautiful girl of 15 when she volunteered directly to General Washington to serve as a messenger. She was eagerly accepted. Disguised as an aged woman she traveled through British lines. She hid messages in many ingenious ways including in bullets under her tongue. On at least one occasion she swallowed the evidence to prevent its seizure.

During the terrible winter at Valley Forge she nursed the sick, and there she met her future husband, Ensign John Davis. He served with Washington from 1777 to 1781. His experiences included carrying the flag when

Washington crossed the Delaware and carrying the wounded Lafayette from the field at Brandywine. He helped care for another injured soldier, James Monroe. He himself was wounded at Bergen Point but stayed in the line. He was partially crippled for life as a result.

John and Ann were married in 1783 and had their nine children in the East. Both were past 50 when they moved to Ohio in 1816. They settled first on several hundred acres at Berkshire, Delaware County, then came to Franklin County. Their big farm lay east of the Scioto and a mile south of Dublin. And that is where they rest today.

It is a tiny cemetery (about 5600 Riverside Drive) east of and now high above the roadway. It may be reached via a set of stone stairs embedded in the bank. Enclosed by ancient stone walls once so common to the area, it is beautifully kept. Most of the headstones are lettered "Davis" but there are also Sells, Wooley, Brelsford, Brunk, Wright and others.

The dominant monument is the imposing freestone one I sketched, guarding the graves of Ann and John, both soldiers and both dead for more than a century. On the sides of the stone are lettered details of their war service. The Ann Simpson Davis Chapter of the DAR has placed a marker at the edge of the road across from the graveyard.

Olentangy Farmhouse

AN OLD history states that Clinton Township was settled as early as 1800—along the west bank of the Whetstone (now Olentangy) River. This choice of sides may have been because a wide floodplain bordered much of the east bank while the land rose steeply quite near the stream's western edge.

General John Rathbone of New York had much of this choice land to sell. He had a grant for 4000 acres (signed by John Adams) for military service. He began selling it off as soon as James Kilbourne of Worthington completed a survey in 1809. A farm of 110 acres went to Obed Blakesley for $442.50—one half down and two years to pay. This handsome home of white brick stands on a last remnant of that farm at what is now 4109 Olentangy River Road.

Blakesley sold most of his land to Amaziah Stanley for a nice profit. Stanley conveyed it to Laura Cook. In 1826 Laura and Rodney Cook secured a loan of $1452 and built the front portion of this house. An unusual condensation of a familiar New England farmhouse style, it dispenses with a center hall and had two front doors instead.

The second, now bricked up, was in the blank space to the right of the remaining door. The stairway rose along a back wall. The present door opened into the big living-kitchen where still may be seen the huge fireplace with its cooking crane in place.

The property changed hands many times, including more and less land. In 1846 it was appraised at $25 an acre for 25 acres, the homestead tract (presumably including the house).

In 1865 it was sold to Joseph Garrett, who put together more than 200 acres known as the Garrett Farm. Edith Knell Reitzel owned it in the 1940s.

Her daughter, Mrs. Thelma Teach, told me the whole family used to bobsled into the valley of Turkey Run just north of the house. Then they enjoyed hot soup kept simmering in a big iron pot hanging from the crane. Mrs. Reitzel planted a number of tiny, foot-high evergreens near the house that are now 30 to 40-foot giants.

In 1950 the house was bought by Professor Everett Schreck. Schreck has been a professional actor on Broadway and, for the past 21 years, professor of theater at Ohio State University. He has written two books on theater (one, *Principles and Styles of Acting,* is to be published next winter) in his pleasant, second-story study. He has just retired from the university. Early next year he will be in Hollywood to act in a movie, Elia Kazan's *The Arrangement.*

The Elkhorn Tavern

ON A DIRECT line between Columbus and Lancaster, and once on the principal road, lies the village of Lithopolis. It was an ideal location for a good tavern, and that, from all accounts, was an understatement for Col. James Hite's Elkhorn Tavern.

Colonel Hite is more fortunate than most men of past glory for having as a great-granddaughter a novelist of note. Minnie Hite Moody, after writing four successful novels, began to research her own ancestry. She became much interested in the colonel and made him the main character in her fifth book, *Long Meadows*. I found it delightful, especially its picture of the little German settlement called Lithopolis for its famous freestone quarries.

Lithopolis was important in the 1820s and the tavern was celebrated among stagecoach travelers. Colonel Hite was a Virginian by way of Kentucky who had fought in the War of 1812 and served as aide and messenger to General Harrison. He came to Lithopolis in 1826 with his family and a retinue of freed slaves to take over the then quite small inn.

Eventually it became a huge affair, some 120 feet in length with vast stables for Hite's own racing horses, those of guests and the stagecoach line's motive power. Fine food and drink and the courtly affability of the host assured success from the start.

"Refreshment for man and beast" began at the long hitching rack in front. There, within reach of the tired horses, was a great stone trough always full of cool water. The colonel had contrived a leaden conduit from a distant, uphill spring to supply tavern and trough. In the cellar, hewed out of a single block of stone, was a second trough which kept milk, butter and other tavern fare cool and fresh.

The Elkhorn had its finest hour in 1840. General, and presidential candidate, William Henry Harrison was campaigning in Columbus when he decided to spurn the glittering Neil House, journey to Lithopolis and stay with his old companion in arms, James Hite. J. H. Galbraith wrote that candidate James Buchanan also stayed at the Elkhorn—in 1856.

The old structure has undergone many changes. Partly razed long ago, its big stables burned in 1890. It has served as a grocery, poolroom and latterly as an ice cream parlor. It was remodeled into apartments recently.

The pair of elkhorns (replaced at least once) that hung above the door are gone. But the homely little belfry, sans bell, still stands as it did when the bell was rung to announce stage arrivals and to call guests to dinner.

One might call my version a "liberty bell" since I took the liberty of restoring it in the drawing.

Cloverhill Place

I 'VE HAD many letters requesting a *Vignette* on this intriguing house. The most recent, from Lucille Schumacher, begins: "Like many 'Hilltoppers' I have long had a great curiosity about the old mansion-type home located on West Mound just west of the Byers car lot on the south side of the street."

Some of my other correspondents used the name that appears beside its steep, winding drive, "Cloverhill Place." With such precise information even I found it with no difficulty. Owner Mary C. Grant was not yet in residence for the summer but Cecil L. Neff who manages her property met me. We toured the house and I learned a little of its history.

The 19th Century was still new when one William Throckmorton was granted this 100 acres for his three years service as a private in "the Virginia Line on Continental Establishment." It was part of the Virginia Military District, land lying northwest of the Ohio River between the Little Miami and the Scioto. William conveyed the land to John Harrison in 1816, and he, for some reason, allowed it to be sold for taxes in 1829.

According to the abstract, it was bought by Adam Brotherlin for the unbelievably small sum of "five dollars, sixty-six cents and four mills." Brotherlin was listed as a tanner residing at 18 High Street in an 1848 directory. That was the year he died and left the property to his

two married daughters. Both of them left it to the daughter of one, Nannie Campbell who married Allen A. Gibson. Their daughter, Mary (Gibson) Grant, the present owner, thus lives on land that has been in her family for 138 years.

A house called Cloverhill has stood on this high point for over a hundred years. The land once stretched east to Mt. Calvary Cemetery (including Jet Stadium site) and west to beyond Central Point Shopping Center. It ran from the center of Trappe Free Pike (now Mound Street) to Green Lawn Cemetery.

After the original house burned, this grander Cloverhill rose in its place. Built in 1885, it abounds in the picturesque detail of the time and has many unusual features: The little latticed gallery off a corner bedroom, where Mary Grant once kept a pet monkey; the grand, theatrical stairway lighted by a big arched window and a row of smaller ones in stained glass; and the combination *portecochere* and deep, cool, sitting porch.

Mary Grant has always needed her spacious estate to keep innumerable pets and riding horses. She inherited her love for horses from her father who used to ride every morning all the way to High Street to get his morning paper. Now High Street is only minutes away, but Cloverhill is so deeply set in its great tree-shaded lawn that it might be in the remotest rural location.

Deshler and Mozart

FRIEDRICH WITTENMEIER was a mighty solid sort of citizen, not at all given to nonsense, and his house at 147 Deshler Avenue reflects this. He was a master stone mason who became one of the leading stone contractors of his day—until the biggest job at the turn of the century broke him.

As a good German-American he couldn't consider any site for his home except the South Side. He bought the choicest lot to be had, at the corner of Deshler and Mozart (now Fourth) facing Schiller Park and only yards from its pretty lake. His daughter, Hertha (Wittenmeier) Laufsweiler, told me about the house, their pleasant life and what a fine man her father was.

It was a big family of 12: Four boys, four girls and two maids. It appears from records that the house was built in 1884, long after flossier styles were in vogue. Only the ornate chimneys reflect those times. But the house was extra modern in some respects, having a fine bath upstairs, lavatory down and its own water system.

The water system was something of a character builder for the boys. It involved a huge tank on the third floor. A big double-acting piston pump in the basement was actuated by a long lever; the "armstrong system" it was sometimes called. It seemed to take hours to fill it. Except for the tank, the top floor was all open and

was where the boys had swings and a roller rink for bad weather.

The two living rooms still have gorgeous mantelpieces of sculptured Italian marble. With their 12-foot ceilings, these are indeed stately rooms.

In summertime the children ran through the park to meet their father who always came that way from his stoneyard on West Mound Street. Friedrich had a favorite seat on the edge of the lake that was always called "father's bench." Here he enjoyed the graceful cruising of the swans whose safety and welfare were his concern.

Behind the house was the big brick stable, connected to the house by a thickly-meshed grape arbor. The mother, Agnes, took pride in her immaculate vegetable and flower garden and tended the egg layers in their chicken house. But in 1913 the mortgaged house was lost. Friedrich had never recovered from disastrous losses when he built the Statehouse Annex in 1901.

For 34 years the house was owned by the George Caskey family and then by several others. It had been converted into several apartments by 1962 when it was bought by Dr. John Stevens. Elizabeth Stevens, whose love for the house is phenomenal, is restoring it to fabulous elegance. When all is complete it may well be the finest example of its period in town.

Note: This piece was originally written in 1957 and published in *The Columbus Dispatch Sunday Magazine*. The late James Thurber has always been my literary hero. Naturally I glory in the fact that he was born and grew up in Columbus. I have also always delighted in the fact that Columbus figures in so many of his stories. It was a real thrill to dig out the locations of the several Thurber homes and places associated with his boyhood. Now, sadly, many of them are gone, including Thurber's birthplace on Parsons Avenue. One of the happiest results of the story was an exchange of letters with Thurber, one of which supplied the material for a Vignette, "Thurber's Ghost House," which appears earlier in this book.

"IN THE early years of the nineteenth century, Columbus won out, as State capital, by only one vote over Lancaster, and ever since then has had the hallucination that it is being followed, a curious municipal state of mind which affects, in some way or another, all those who live there."

That fragment of the prose of James Grover Thurber, of dubious historical accuracy, has been called "one of the funniest and also one of the most imaginative sentences in English." The sweeping judgment was made by no less an authority than Clifton Fadiman.

Other critics have other favorite Thurber sentences — there are thousands of likely candidates. The Columbus resident may be gladdened (or saddened, depending on his temperament) to know that some of the funniest involve Columbus.

Thurber's birthplace, at 251 Parsons Avenue, is now gone.

All over America and in all parts of the world are people who know Columbus principally as the town where Thurber found such weird and wonderful goings-on in the early years of this century. Visitors from England, where Thurber is almost worshiped, count Columbus a major literary shrine.

In 1953, *Thurber Country*, 17th book by J.G.T., was published amid the glad cries of his admirers, David McCord wrote in *Saturday Review of Literature*, "May the day never come when Thurber Country yields to the bulldozer and the ranch house. There is still, fortunately for all of us, but a single covered wagon creaking across it. The driver is a former Ohio State man, as he should be. I fear that he may acknowledge a little loneliness at times. But if it is any compensation to him he ought to know by now that he is the greatest and most original humorist this country has produced to date."

If Thurber Country is a strange land without geographic boundaries, Thurbertown is easily located on any map, roughly at the center of the state of Ohio.

Fact and fancy become mixed when Jim Thurber writes of his home town. The plodding researcher falls back on more sober histories, old city directories and the memories of friends to sort out facts. For instance, in the preface to one of his books, "James Thurber was born on a night of wild portent and high wind, in the year of 1894, at 147 Parsons Avenue, Columbus, Ohio." The city directory for that portentious year gives the Thurber family residence as 251 Parsons Avenue, a matter of a hundred yards down the avenue.

"The house, which is still standing, bears no tablet or plaque of any description, and is never pointed out to visitors. Once Thurber's mother, walking past the place

Another Thurber residence, at 921 South Champion, where Mary Thurber once collected 16 dogs.

with an old lady from Fostoria, Ohio, said to her, 'My son James was born in that house,' to which the old lady, who was extremely deaf, replied, 'Why on the Tuesday morning train, unless my sister is worse.' Mrs. Thurber let it go at that." Thus the author disposes of his birthplace. There was a plaque (or placard rather) at 251 when I visited there recently. Its laconic inscription, "For Sale."

"The infant Thurber was brought into the world by an old practical nurse named Margery Albright, who had delivered the babies of neighbor women before the Civil War."

Aunt Margery, as the young James Thurber called her, figured largely in the little boy's life and later in his writings. His first literary effort (still held over his head by his brother Robert) was a poetic effusion to her remarkable garden. "It was a narrow plot . . . that began with an elephant ear near the rickety wooden fence in front and extended to the trellis of moonflowers against the wall of Jim West's stable. It was further shaded by her own house and the Fenstermakers' and it caught only stingy glimpses of the sun, but, to the wonder of the jubrous, it sustained for forty summers Canterbury bells and bluebells, bleeding hearts and fuchsias, asters and roses . . . 'This garden,' said Dr. Sparks, pastor of the old Third Street Methodist Church, one day, 'is a testament of faith.' 'It takes faith, and it takes work, and it takes a lot of good, rich manure," said Mrs. Albright, far and away the most distinguished manurist of her time . . . "

Aunt Margery has been honored in Thurber's magnificent tribute, "Daguerreotype of a Lady." She emerges a titan of early Columbus womanhood, a healer superior to all her doctor contemporaries and a coiner of wonderful words — *jubrious* for dubious; *whinker,* a combination of whinny and whicker and *naushy* for nausea.

Mrs. Albright's home was the north half of a frame double that once stood at 185 South Fifth Street. The house and the wonderful garden are gone, but the spreading sycamore, allowed by a "genial city council" to grow in the middle of the brick sidewalk, is still there. Thurber's fondest childhood memories center on the location. He wrote in one of his books that the site was now occupied by a filling station and that the tree was gone. It may please him to know he was mistaken, that the empty lot is still shaded by the fine old tree.

Among the many homes of his boyhood that Thurber mentions, "77 Lexington Avenue" occurs most frequently. It develops that his phenomenal memory for trivia is at fault. The correct address is 77 Jefferson Avenue. It is the locale of his stories, "The Night the Ghost Got In" and "More Alarms at Night," incredible, past-bedtime stories which have greatly enriched our literature.

The cast in these stories includes Thurber's mother and father and two brothers. The brothers, both Columbus residents, are Robert C. and William F. Thurber. In the stories their identity is gallantly, if thinly, concealed by the pseudonyms "Roy and Herman."

In 1949, according to one of Thurber's stories, he engaged in a losing battle of correspondence with a book publisher over a consignment of unordered books, *Grandma Was a Nudist*. He wrote to the publisher with special scorn, "It would not surprise me if your firm or some other publisher, wrote me in care of my mother at 568 Oak Street . . . I was thirteen years old when we lived there, back in 1908."

Thurber home at 568 Oak Street is now gone.

The sarcasm was wasted, it appeared, for the books were promptly shipped to the Oak Street address to the great discomfiture of the 1949 resident.

One of Thurber's favorite homes was at 921 South Champion Avenue. He wrote, "When we lived there in 1899 and 1900 it was the last house on the street. Just south of us the avenue dwindled to a wood road that led into a thick grove of oak and walnut trees, long since destroyed by the southward march of asphalt. Our nearest neighbor on the north was fifty yards away, and across from us was a country meadow."

It was at 921 that Mary Thurber, Jim's mother, created a mighty diversion on the occasion of Aunt Mary Van York's visit. Aunt Mary was an outspoken dog-hater, a fact probably resented by the dog-loving Thurbers. In any case, Mrs. Thurber collected and incarcerated in their basement some 16 dogs prior to Aunt Mary's arrival. Somehow she persuaded that worthy lady to carry a plate of food to the head of the basement stairs for the two Thurber dogs.

When the door was opened the charge of the dog brigade was all that could have been hoped for. Aunt Mary, backed into a corner, screamed, "Great God Almighty! It's a dog factory." Then she proceeded to clean house and thus closed another chapter in Life with the Thurbers.

This house, at 695 Bryden Road, was the home of Thurber's grandfather and a "wonderful play place."

Of all the houses Thurber loved, none is remembered more fondly than 695 Bryden Road, the home of his commission-merchant grandfather, William M. Fisher. Grandfather Fisher built the fine old house, the first on Bryden Road, in 1884.

"Until twenty years after Gettysburg," Thurber writes, "Town Street had not ventured past Parsons Avenue, an eastern boundary of polite, middle-class living marked by a tall oak left standing in the middle of the street. Here Town Street suddenly took a jog to the right, as if to avoid the old tree, and proceeded east under its fancy name of Bryden Road. My grandfather owned the first three lots on the right and built his house across from the grounds of what is now the Columbus School for Girls."

The house still stands, much changed by the removal of its four rambling porches, but the school has removed to its new Bexley home.

Number 695 Bryden is presently occupied by physicians. To verify the location I asked one of the doctors' receptionists if the house had been the Fisher home.

"I don't know," she answered, "but that crazy cartoonist once lived here."

I tried to think what "crazy cartoonist" it might have been. Giving up I explained that I was interested in the Fishers because they were grandparents to James Thurber.

"Thurber!" she exclaimed. "That's who I mean — that crazy cartoonist."

Robert Thurber says that his family did live there briefly in 1912 but James remembers it as his grandparents' home and a wonderful play place for the children of the clan. "There were seven bedrooms . . . and the place seemed to us grandchildren designed for games of hide and seek."

The granite carriage stone marked "Fisher 1884" is gone from its place in front of the old house, but the name Fisher and the date 1870 appear on a Town Street building between Third and Fourth Streets. It frowns down from an ornate cornice on the confused activity of the commission house district of which it has been a part for more than three-quarters of a century.

This, too, was a favorite place in Thurbertown. "You walked into a dark, cool place smelling richly of fruits and vegetables. In one room were enormous wooden bins filled with a million nuts, and kegs of grapes from Spain. Two or three black cats prowled softly about looking for

mice, and occasionally we saw the darting figure of a
ferret that had been installed in the store to fight off rats.
In another and colder room, lighted by flaring gas jets in
the years of my earliest memories, bunches of bananas
hung from the ceiling...We were always a little scared
in this room, because big, hairy tarrantulas were occasionally found among the bananas, which came from Honduras
and Guatemala."

*The produce house of Thurber's grandfather, William M.
Fisher. It was on Town Street between Third and Fourth.*

The Fisher home on Bryden backed up to the old
blind school at Parsons and Main. Young Thurber spent
a lot of time playing on the grounds and watching spirited
contests that took place on the ball field. The school baseball team, captained by Frank James, played on "the
craziest baseball field in the history of the game."

"The main building sent back two brown wings or
tentacles...the left tentacle crept up to within fifty feet
of the second baseman, and the other swung behind the
center fielder, forcing him to play in and cramping the
range of his action. The blunt end of this wing was separated from the stables by thirty feet of paved courtyard, on
which the left fielder had to stand, an easy victim of rico-
cheting balls, frightened horses and stablemen with pitch-
forks. If these were the stony frustrations of a Freudian
dream, the gigantic tree between first and second was a
hazard out of Lewis Carroll.

"It had the patriarchal spread of Longfellow's chest-
nut and it could drop leaves on the shortstop and, with its
large and sinewy roots, trip up runners rounding first.

*The old State School for the Blind on East Main Street was the
site of "the craziest baseball field."*

Many a hard-hit ball that should have been good for extra
bases would cling and linger in the thick foliage of that
ancient tree, and drop finally into Frank James' glove, or
the glove of the right fielder who had plenty of time to
jog in from his position on the concrete walk beside the
left wing and wait for it to come down. Visiting players
screamed and cursed . . . Sometimes the finicky enemy
would quit in disgust, late in the game, after the James
Boys had demonstrated a special and practiced skill in
bouncing balls off the walls, losing it on roofs, hitting it

into the crotch of the tree, or lining it under the lowest
bough, so that it would land on the concrete pavement and
roll to Parsons Avenue, a hundred and fifty yards away."

Among those whom Thurber mentions as playing on
the blind school grounds are Billy Alloway, Billy South-
worth, Hank Gowdy and Billy Purtell. In football season,
such later greats as Chick Harley, Allen and Johnny Thurman and Raymond Eichenlaub played there.

In his story, " I Went to Sullivant," Thurber tells
about his years (1900-1908) at Sullivant School. Sullivant, he said was "tough" and had one of the greatest baseball teams in the city. "Several of its best players were in
the fourth grade, known to the teachers of the school as the
Terrible Fourth...Some of the more able players had
been in the fourth grade for seven or eight years...The
dean of the squad was a tall, husky young man of twenty-
two who was in the fifth grade."

"The Sullivant School baseball team of 1905 defeated
several high school teams in the city and claimed the high
school championship of the state...Their road season was
called off after a terrific fight that occurred during a game
in Mt. Sterling or Piqua or Xenia (the battle continued on
down into the business section of the town and raged for
hours with much destruction of property) but since Sullivant was ahead 17 to 0 there could have been no doubt
as to the outcome...All of us boys were sure our team

*This was old Sullivant School, on East State between Fifth and
Sixth, where Thurber went to school.*

could have beaten Ohio State University that year, but
they wouldn't play us; they were scared."

Thurber continued to live in and store up memories
about Columbus until 1924. He attended Ohio State University where he came under the strong influence of Joseph
Russell Taylor, professor of English and extravagant ad-
mirer of Henry James. If, as has been remarked, Thurber's
writing has Jamesian qualities, Joe Taylor was probably
responsible. Thurber's "Man With a Pipe" is his substantial thanks to a teacher he loved above the others.

After a short time wartime stint as a code clerk in
the American Embassy in Paris, Thurber came back to
Columbus and became a reporter on *The Columbus Dispatch*, which he called "a fat and amiable newspaper,
whose city editor seldom knew where I was and got so he
didn't care."

To commemorate the 150th anniversary of Ohio's beginnings as a state, a special Ohioana Sesquicentennial
medal was prepared and presented to James Thurber. The
honored author responded with great modesty and concluded, "I have lived in the East for nearly thirty years
now, but many of my books prove that I am never very
far away from Ohio in my thoughts, and that the clocks
that strike in my dreams are often the clocks of Columbus.
They have never struck a finer hour for me than this one."

INDEX